SAGE HUNTRESS LOVER QUEEN

Access Your Power and Creativity through Sacred Female Archetypes

MARA BRANSCOMBE

FINDHORN PRESS

Findhorn Press
One Park Street
Rochester, Vermont 05767
www.findhornpress.com

Text stock is SFI certified

Findhorn Press is a division of Inner Traditions International

Disclaimer
The information in this book is given in good faith and intended for
information only. Neither author nor publisher can be held liable by
any person for any loss or damage whatsoever which may arise from
the use of this book or any of the information therein.

Cataloging-in-Publication data for this title is available from the Library of Congress

ISBN 978-1-64411-793-4 (print)
ISBN 978-1-64411-794-1 (ebook)

Printed and bound in the United States by Lake Book Manufacturing, LLC
The text stock is SFI certified. The Sustainable Forestry Initiative® program
promotes sustainable forest management.

10 9 8 7 6 5 4 3 2 1

Edited by Jane Ellen Combelic
Illustrations by Laura Mowbray
Text design and layout by Anna-Kristina Larsson
This book was typeset in Garamond and Gill Sans.

To send correspondence to the author of this book, mail a first-class letter
to the author c/o Inner Traditions • Bear & Company, One Park Street,
Rochester, VT 05767, USA and we will forward the communication,
or contact the author directly at **www.marabranscombe.com**

SAGE, HUNTRESS, LOVER, QUEEN

"*Sage, Huntress, Lover, Queen* is a beautiful guide that leads to a deeper understanding of self. Through the teachings of powerful archetypes, Mara's wisdom activates a remembering of who we are and why we are here. This book spoke deeply to the visionary, the healer, and the matriarch within my bones, and I highly recommend it to anyone who wishes to continue weaving their medicine into the world."

~ **ASHA FROST,** indigenous medicine woman
and author of *You Are the Medicine*

"Mara Branscombe mystically and masterfully weaves rituals, poetry, somatic practices, meditations, and movement throughout the pages of *Sage, Huntress, Lover, Queen* to inspire deep transformation. This book is an ever-expanding and rich portal for uncovering and revealing what must come forth from one's Soul for their own healing and the healing that is and must continue to take place collectively."

~ **MICHELLE C. JOHNSON,** intuitive healer, activist, and author of
Skill in Action: Radicalizing Your Yoga Practice to Create a Just World
and *Finding Refuge: Heart Work for Healing Collective Grief*

"There is healing in these pages. As we journey through the archetypes, we reclaim our power and sojourn with all of the parts of ourselves that are ready for healing, rebirth, and renewal."

~ **TRACEE STANLEY,** founder of Empowered Life Circle
and author of *Radiant Rest* and *The Luminous Self*

"Mara's words are true homecoming for the feminine. To read it is to remember. This book invites us to reclaim our power and restore what we have lost and forgotten. A deep and satiating read."

~ **ALLY MAZ,** entrepreneur, yoga teacher, and author of *Girlvana*

"Thank you, Mara, for giving women a map to explore the power of archetypes to embody the many dimensions of our full spectrum. Each chapter offers juicy practices, prose, and poetry to embrace the fullness of one's life through the feminine lens while meeting the shadows that arise along the way. An empowerment offering for these soulful times."

~ **SHIVA REA,** international yoga teacher and
author of *Tending the Heart Fire*

"Mara Branscombe is passionately committed to inspiring each reader to live the most empowered, creative, and authentic life possible. She goes far beyond her own beautiful words of inspiration as she provides an abundance of practical tools (meditation, journaling, rituals, and more) for the genuine seeker to use to immerse herself in an active physical/emotional/spiritual exploration of any or all of the seven sacred female archetypes highlighted in *Sage, Huntress, Lover, Queen.* Branscombe links the weaving of personal accountability and divine feminine wisdom to the urgent necessity of bringing healing to our world in this sincere and encouraging call to awakening."

~ **ROBIN ROSE BENNETT,** herbalist and author of
Healing Magic and *The Gift of Healing Herbs*

"Mara's latest book, *Sage, Huntress, Lover, Queen,* reads almost like a map helping you understand your inner-world, while navigating the outer one. Poetic, insightful, and deeply practical, Mara helps you understand the transitions in life through a compelling and original look at the archetypes. This book provides equal amounts of practical information with a wisdom that seems almost otherworldly."

~ **ALLY BOGARD,** teacher and cofounder of
Gaiatri Yoga Training Program

This book is dedicated to the heart and soul change-makers of the world—for the divine feminine is calling us to remember who we are and why we are here.

May the sacred feminine whisper again and again— you are worthy, you are whole, you are love.

"It's a wonderful day,
I have never seen this one before."

Maya Angelou

WEAVE

Contents

Chapter 6 – Awakening the Mystic

Truth Seeker, Vision Holder, Divine Space Explorer

Chapter 7 – The Queen

Knowledge Weaver, Vision Activator, Evolved Leader

Introduction
Evoking the Divine Feminine Way,
Revealing the Archetypes

Inside the quiet company of your beloved self,
count your blessings.
Untangle the weight of worldly complexities
long enough to breathe, and deeply.
Like the visionary on her soul-retrieving journey,
gather the architecture inside your universal metamorphosis.
We are building now.
There is momentum.

No longer run from the guilty-shamed-buried-deep-dark secrets,
rather let them bubble up your spine and spill like forgotten
sacred texts out of your mouth.
Be a channel for the mythic night sky;
the moon's revolution pulsates within.
Accept the invitation to be a child of this
miraculous earth's wild soul.

Be maiden, mother, sage, huntress, lover, mystic, queen.
You are of this ancient composition.
The homecoming is your evolution.

What would happen if you greeted every day of your life as a creative, intentional, and ceremonial adventure? What would it feel like to go to bed every evening knowing that you are doing good work based on your soul's mission? Satisfied, ready to let go for a good night's rest and be fully restored?

This is your wake-up call to live your precious life infused with joy, seeking truth, dancing with your shadows, and loving fearlessly.

Are you ready to embark upon this path?

Are you ready to finally give yourself back the life you know is yours to live? Are you ready to discover where lack, scarcity, and fear are holding you back? Are you ready to transform the shadows that haunt you? Are you willing to do the personal work it takes to liberate yourself from the roller coaster inside your mind that crushes your worth and keeps you playing small in your life?

Are you ready to say yes to joy over fear, love over hatred, and grace over hardship?

You have picked up this book for a reason. You are here to receive inspiration, practical insight, and spiritual mind–body deepening on the next steps of your personal journey. It's time to nurture and nourish your shadows—to bring them forward as an unearthing process for personal healing. Doing this will also contribute to the collective healing that is necessary for the planet. Everything in life is connected. Your muses and teachers are everywhere around you. The world is rapidly evolving: Witness the waves of global and environmental shifts. How is your personal consciousness evolving? Inside this complex human experience, how are you taking care of yourself?

You have everything you need inside of you now to reveal this cycle of your soul's calling. Observing, naming, and nurturing your shifting consciousness becomes the creative pursuit. The seeds of lasting transformation grow like wildflowers when planted with embodied joy, clear intention, and untamed, uncensored personal expression.

It's time to share your unique gifts with the world. This is the call of the modern visionary, the feminine way fully alive—empowered to the core, fueled by compassion, and anchored deep within the true self.

Feminine Archetypes:
Understanding Self and Reclaiming Wholeness

So, where do we begin on this journey? How can we connect with this personal reclaiming energy and begin our unique self-transformation process?

This book will take you on a creative adventure through the lens of seven female archetypes—Maiden, Mother, Sage, Huntress, Mystic, Lover, and Queen.

The psychoanalyst Carl Jung used the concept of archetype in his theory of the human psyche—including the ego, soul, and self. Jung believed that universal and mythic archetypes live within the collective unconscious. These archetypes represent fundamental human motifs of the individual experience and evolution: patterns or models of characteristics that are repeated throughout the universe.

Exploring the archetypes of Maiden, Mother, Sage, Huntress, Mystic, Lover, and Queen will support you to understand the patterns and behaviors inside your current self—all the while revealing how and why you form relationships, choose careers, and digest mind–body processes. Ultimately, we are a combination of all the female archetypes and can access each one at any stage of life. When we can also incorporate and infuse the elements—earth, water, fire, air, and ether—into the alchemy of our healing mediums, we generate an infinite source of energy.

The archetypes provide an open canvas that you can use to awaken intuition and understand how your mind works. The creator inside you will reveal the past narratives and present-moment activations to help you attune to living life like a creative adventure. The unbounded wisdom contained within the archetypes will deeply support your journey. Like reflection points inside the compass of your experience, you will receive striking epiphanies revealing where you are, where you are going, and how to get where you want to be.

It's time to call in the energy you desire. It's time to live the life that has been waiting for you. It's time to burn the limiting roles, smash the preconceived boxes, and liberate yourself from societal norms and trauma of the past. Like gateways into a deeper understanding of self on the path towards freedom, may the archetypal insights and practices in this book form an inspiring, creative journey for personal and collective healing. Understanding and embodying these portals will trigger an archetypal response and naturally, with commitment and curiosity, activate a return to your essential self.

Lean into what brings you limitless joy.
Dwell in the company of people and practices that inspire you.
Forgive often.
Pray daily.
Bask in nature's finest details.
Listen to the birds sing.
Sunbathe, ocean dip, forest walk.
Begin again.
Fall freely, dance wildly.
Grace will catch you.
Honor your desires.
Make art over war.
Drink in the quiet moments.
Return to your holy body as a vessel of compassion.
Witness the wildflowers bloom in the most rugged conditions.

The Wisdom Inside the Feminine Archetypes
Maiden: Underworld Explorer

Wildly magnetic, authentic to the core, the maiden's passionate approach to life is infectious. But her shadow keeps her stuck in people-pleasing paradigms, distorts her sense of innocence, and robs her of her youthful spirit and creative power.

Learn how to unlock fear-based choices; how to ignite your sense of purpose through creativity, forgiveness, and courage—this is the maiden's homecoming.

Mother Earth: Matrix

The mother archetype is steady, abundant, and holds a positive life-giving force in all her actions. Her shadow comes through as over-giving, co-dependent, and depleted.

Learn how to embrace a radical self-love to heal body-image trauma, release lack, and generate abundance. Heal your mother's ancestral line and allow the earth mothership within you to finally flourish.

Sage: Water Healer

The wisdom of the sage archetype streams through the development, discernment, and transformative abilities inside her emotional process. Her healing power and intuitive channels flow through the element of water.

The sage's shadow work is to no longer hide her true emotions, to feel connected to her community and experience her sense of belonging in the world.

Learn how to transform wounds into wisdom and accept the full expression of your emotions as a superpower, not a weakness.

Huntress: Fire Generator

The huntress fully embodies the warrior spirit. She knows her worth and unapologetically shares it with the world. She intuits when to activate her visions and how to push through challenges. Her confidence allows her to follow through with her life goals.

The huntress's shadow avoids vulnerability and tends to rely on herself entirely to complete her life's mission.

Find your true inner power, shed old egoic body and mind narratives that make you play small in life. Discover how to wisely fuel your intentions, passion projects, and dreams to avoid burnout.

Lover: Air Alchemist

The lover embraces infinite confidence and sensuality to its fullest capacity. Her mission in life is to experience the deepest forms of intimacy possible.

The lover's shadow shows up in the ways she creates and attaches to drama in her relationships.

Learn how to adore and adorn your body to meet the goddess you are. Receive insight into where you push away intimacy in fear of exposing your true self. Overcome fear of intimacy, dismantle the complexities inside your relationships, and activate the deeply satisfying nature of the embodied, sensual lover.

Mystic: Ethereal Time Traveller

An alchemist of spirit and magic, the mystic is an advocate for self-sovereignty and can access higher levels of consciousness through her intuitive gifts. Her work is to release self-judgement to be a clear channel to both the human and spiritual planes.

Unearth your inner healer and shed toxic build-up that is blocking your potential to evolve in body, mind, and spirit. Develop your intuitive channels and share your unique voice with the world.

Queen: Universal Thought Weaver

The queen's perspective is vast and wide. She understands where she needs to put her energy to get what she wants in life. She makes bold decisions for the betterment of humanity. Her shadow lurks in her attachment to perfectionism, being overly critical, and always needing to be right.

Learn how to mature your leadership by accepting faults in yourself and others. Dismantle the overbearing desire for perfectionism and refine the voice of the higher self to be channeled through to your external expressions. Letting go to let in truth and knowledge is the queen's work.

Living with the Archetypes

Each archetype is a steppingstone on the winding river of life's great adventures. To reclaim faith and embrace life as a living ceremony, an adventurous journey, a wild heart experience, an awakened sense of mystery, and a remembering of magic is to embody this precious life you have been given. The feminine archetypes will support you in every single process, at every stage of your life. It is like the recipe handed down from your spirit grandmother—you are supported, you are not alone, you are ready for this journey. You are ready to evolve into the intuitive and life-giving feminine force that is uniquely yours.

Guided by the insight of soul work within the archetypal lens, enhanced by daily creative pursuits and perspective shifts, the embodied divine feminine reclaims her birthright towards wholeness, worth, and a wild, adventurous life force. She walks the path of inquiry, depth, joy, and soul purpose.

The visionary in you is alive and awake to the creative compass within. Navigating, tracking, planning, and seeing all experiences—past, present, and future—as vital steps across the river of her life journey. Her ultimate destination is freedom to live the life she knows aligns with her soul essence. The intuitive within understands that both her shadows and her light forces are her greatest tools and her most essential resources. Walk your newfound freedom home into the joy-infused, soul-retrieved life that is authentically yours.

Change as the Path and the Process

As we evolve and travel through a multitude of life experiences—from highs to lows, joy to struggle, from love stories to the deepest grief—inevitably the course of our life alters, and we change. And yet, planted within the core of every life experience is a seed of wisdom. How we respond to change in our life becomes the gateway towards leading a clear, purposeful, and joyful existence. It's not what happens to us in life, it's how we become the embodied creator in response. Working with past experiences as the creative material and with intuitive seeds in the present is the gateway towards greater freedom—physically, spiritually, emotionally, and intellectually.

Our experiences are both unique and unpredictable. If we resist, repress, or deny the inner shifts that want to be expressed—whether they be large or small—we turn away before we have a chance to see through the window. As we age, we begin to observe more clearly how these changes are inevitable. Our physical body changes, our emotional reactions shift, our mental process deepens, and our spiritual life matures. In essence, we have an opportunity to navigate our life with fierce grace, endless joy, and an epic sea of compassion. Yet, if we block our ability to stay present to these shifts and shut down parts of us that are meant to evolve, we become burdened, hardened, dehydrated, unloved, disconnected, and uninspired in life.

The Essential Self

Life in this age of technology, multi-tasking, and never-ending expectations of doing and being more has raised the bar for us. Realizing our whole, balanced, and connected feminine energy has become a struggle, unattainable and exhausting. A powerful way to distill and refine the essential self is to embody both the fullness and the shadow inside the divine feminine archetypal cycles.

Are you ready for the journey home to your most essential self?

The reclamation of the true *self* makes you unique in the world. You can unearth, sculpt, and align with the gifts and challenges you were born with, and allow them to enhance your quality of life. Perhaps you will realize the power of saying no after so many years of not knowing how to, or the grace of finally saying yes—I am ready for this life transformation. It's time to explore how to fully express the truth of who you are through a creative, feminine, and wildly transformative lens.

By working with the archetypal and elemental pillars, we begin to understand why patterns repeat themselves and why we continue to play out habitual paradigms. Instead, we can walk the path towards inner union. We can create deep-seated connections to all the people in our lives.

When the feminine archetypes are revealed, we can go further into our own personal inquiry and inner listening journey. We sense the shadows ready to be seen, acknowledged, and worked through. We relate more deeply to ourselves and our communities. We place our awareness in the humble seat of the beginner; the inner child is ready, curious, and awakened to connect in a more vulnerable way.

If these archetypal pillars are not explored, worked with, and digested, they will not become embodied. The shadows of unworthiness, shame, guilt, fear, anger, and trauma will continue to haunt you, hold you back, and numb your experience.

The mission is to reclaim your lost, wounded, and repressed patterns. It is your birthright to live in a way that is unapologetically you—wild, free, peaceful, joyous, steady, and spirited all at once. The world is ready for you to express your true feelings and cast your soul gifts far and wide. When you answer the call to dive in and commit to embodying the divine feminine, you have arrived on the healing path of the future. It becomes a lifelong study of compassionate living and authentic loving. Every day becomes both an adventure and a ceremony. This is how dreams come alive.

Feed the center of your universe with a steady, magnetic attention.
Pay attention long enough and you will see that
this is where the magic dwells.

There will always be challenges, change, and the unknown.
And yet, the sun continues to bless you through it all. Build your
capacity to maneuver life's wild rides. From the darkest nights to
the brightest days, feed the center of your universe with gold.

Bow to humility.
Rise to forgiveness.
Allow compassion to be your teacher.
For if not you, then who?
For if not here, then where?
Let joy in when it surges through your blood
and makes your heart skip a beat.
Love from the core of your body.
Follow the sun's lead. No longer dim your light.
You are worthy of your greatest dreams.
The world is ready for your creative, wild, and courageous self.

Shifting Consciousness: Embodying the Feminine Way

Now is the time to weave the wisdom of the feminine into an embodiment of leadership, love, and right action. We are being drawn to shift our consciousness—to discern, see, feel, question, and sense everything in a new way. The time has come to raise the human vibration to evolve alongside our current shape-shifting environment.

There is a resonance within the feminine channel that is calling us to align, wake up, and live in a reciprocal way with nature, humans, animals, and ourselves. To no longer battle, push, force, or plough through life without deepening into our true nature. When we encourage our passions and core values to stream through us, we create less inner conflict, and in turn, generate a higher vibrational life experience. A movement towards an embodied soul love and leadership through the feminine lens merges, ignites, and forever shifts one's consciousness for the betterment of humanity.

Let us see beyond the past definition of male or female into a universal consciousness of goodness and right action. The path of the new feminine way is a shift away from our current political, social, and economical structures. The imbalance created by the old structures is calling for a radical shift.

The planet is begging us to wake up. Can you feel it?

Sourcing from the natural world in a reciprocal way allows us to walk hand in hand with nature. This is the feminine way—inclusive, creative, intelligent, efficient, sustainable, and emotionally attuned. With knowledge of the historical systems that have been in place for centuries, we can now discern what works and what doesn't. How would you like to organize your life in this new feminine way? What would you choose as a code of values and ethics free of dominating, patriarchal, racist, sexist, and limiting systems of greed, non-inclusivity, and judgement?

The practice of self-love and love for others may be the most complex, committed, and enduring task of one's life. To put the work into self-realization through embodiment to mature, ripen, and respond to one another is to become a channel for love from wholeness, not from lack. When we trust and understand that we all belong to one another, our capacity for compassion and resilience grows. Our consciousness moves beyond the egoic self into a vast and fluid evolutionary perspective. To discover true belonging within becomes the ultimate quest. This is how we stay authentic, connected, and inspired to walk hand in hand with our higher self in this lifetime.

Be here now on this earth to celebrate the beauty you see in a stranger's eyes, smell the sacred inside the heirloom rose, feel the ancient legacy in the starry night sky, merge with the glimmers of sun that dance upon the still lake. Feel the beauty inside your own pulsing heart, unite with the delicate force of earth, air, fire, water, and ether. Honor your body as the sacred temple in which you journey into the wonders of this precious life. Bask in solitude long enough to hear the voices within that beckon you to share love, joy, and connection from the physical to the unseen spiritual realms. Belonging is what humanity craves. Discovering purpose is the journey. Honoring authentic identity and creativity expression is the process. Gratitude every step of the way is the channel.

At the precipice of the sacred rivers, bow to the holy mountains and the infinite skies, dance with the unknown, and welcome life's great mysteries. Call out your questions to your teachers both on the physical plane and the spiritual plane. Ask for guidance every morning. How can I direct my energy to be in the flow of my gifts and purpose? How can I steady myself to reveal the life teachings at this time? Over time, these questions will open channels for you to receive the answers. You will be guided.

Discover the call of the new feminine way through the archetypal portals. Allow your creative channels to merge, flow, and evolve within your own inner *Maiden, Mother, Sage, Huntress, Lover, Mystic, and Queen. You hold the Weaver's alchemy within you, ready to call upon each archetype as needed, ready to thrive within each stage and cycle in life.*

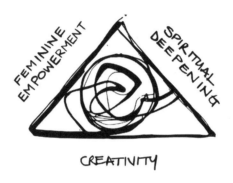

CREATIVITY

Creative Channels Alive

Awakening your creative channels connects you with your empowered, aligned, and true self. Practicing the art of creativity daily, supported by mindful and soul-infused techniques will enhance your emotional well-being and spiritual connectivity.

Revealing the complexities and the shadows within your inner matrix while recognizing the life you truly desire is the healing balm inside this wild adventure.

We are both nature and nurture. We are both stardust and mud. We are both masculine and feminine. We are both sun and moon. When opposing energies, trauma, drama, elations, epiphanies, and past experiences are understood and held in compassion, we are on the healing path. This is the work: to be present to the next stage of empowerment and embodied wholeness through honest, authentic, and anchored personal practices.

How to Use This Book

Staying curious and open-minded is the key to this adventure. Having your own journal alongside this book will support your exploration throughout the elemental and archetypal landscape. Your experience will be personal, unique, and intuitive. I invite you to let go of all your preconceived ideas of who you think you are—including the negative self-talk, the boxes you put yourself in, the faults you see in yourself, and your attachments to your personal struggles. To lay these labels down is the first step towards creative freedom and a reclamation of your essential nature.

Each chapter of *Sage, Huntress, Lover, Queen* presents the timeless characteristics of an archetype through prose, poetry, and creative musings. Mindful and somatic experiences are offered with the intention of integrating body sensations, mind activity, and the sacred realms. Practices such as breathing techniques, movement patterns, creative dates, journal prompts, and guided visualizations further the experience of developing your essential self within each archetype. You may want to read through the whole chapter first and then go back and journal, practice the exercises offered, and receive the guided visualizations in a way that deepens your experience.

The formulas, practices, and remedies in this book are based on my own life experiences interpreted through the female archetypes. After two decades of research and development in the use of somatic practices to tap into the essential self, my inquiry into the shadow and the light of each feminine energy became fuel for my creative pursuits. Through a steady commitment to the practices and teachings of yoga, meditation, and movement, as well as elemental, shamanic, pagan, and earth-centric rituals, the template of the female archetypes ignited a passion inside me for excavating and inspiring the empowered and embodied feminine way home.

Throughout this process, you may be asked to slow down or speed up, to let go or shift your perspective. Archetypal paradigms will be the map, the explorer within will be your guide. Personal affirmations will land inside your center like a cosmic, evocative, and radically liberating experience. Colors will shift, sounds will transform, you will smell the roses in a new way, your touch will become sacred, your gait steady, your breath full. As you reclaim your sense of adventure and enhance your creative approach to life, your thoughts will mirror this inner transformation.

~

Evolve into Freedom: A Visualization

Open your imagination in this moment. Picture yourself laying down your life experiences as if they were treasured sculptures or artifacts. Each story in your living museum holds a different piece of your past. As you begin to place them with intention, you liberate yourself from their pain and their definition of you.

This becomes the living ritual of the inner mystic, huntress, lover, maiden, mother, sage, and queen within.

You clear your energy field from past and future attachments. You generate space for spontaneity and creativity to become your guides in this wild and wondrous life. Your true essence alchemizes through each cycle. Trust the process by freeing the pieces that are ready to evolve. Distill the wisdom received. A new narrative begins.

Your intuition does not arrive with a backstory.
Rather, it emerges through your body like a soft butterfly
wing, a pulse, a surge—like a lightning bolt. A deep inhale
that stops you in your tracks. Yes, these intuitive moments feel
right. They do not feel complex, or come from life's dramas.
They hold a visceral embodiment of a big, bold yes.

A Fine Silk Weave:
Reclaiming Your Feminine Power

Like a fine silk weave, the empowered characteristics of the female archetypes become soul inspiration for intuitive living and compassionate loving. The core message returns to life as a sacred, living ritual.

The maiden's infectious zest, the mother's abundance, the sage's healing powers, the huntress's warrior spirit, the mystic's intuitive capacity, the lover's fearless sensuality, and the queen's clear channel for inner power and wisdom—explore and integrate these characteristics to enhance the quality of your life.

The archetypal artist sees each day as an original creative process. You will tend to the inner child, learn through the lens of curiosity, walk the path of light and dark, and balance inner strength with inner softness. Engage your intuitive capacity through silence, steadiness, and wonderment. No longer fear being alone. Smash the societal paradigms that keep you circling in life decisions and directions that no longer serve you. The ongoing, infinite practice of deep listening, attuning mind–body channels towards wholeness, and welcoming the glimmers of spiritual awakening become your life compass.

Welcome your inner artist to come alive. To love deeply is to surrender to the path of the unknown while creating each day anew. Practicing embodied communication, connection, and wholeness is the process and the path.

The fine silk weave of your empowered feminine spirit is ready to rise and be expressed as the soul song that is uniquely yours—the world is ready to embrace the symphony of your spirit. Now is the time for your unique essence to emerge and to activate personal and collective freedom.

A Blessing for Love through All Life's Stages and Cycles

To the tender inner child, the holy mother within,
and the wise elder who sits before us.
For our mothers, fathers, daughters, sons, sisters, brothers, aunties,
uncles, grandmothers, grandfathers.
To the creators, change-makers, to the quiet and the loud.
To our soul friends who listen, embrace, and love every ounce of us.
For those who have imprinted their memory into our hearts.
We are all caretakers of this sacred legacy.
Carry this forward, and when lost, get lost freely.
And when grief and hardship bring you to the bellows of the earth,
surrender.

Rest there until you are ready.
Like a newly planted seed, you will break ground.
Complexity is not to be feared.
What awaits—no one will ever know.
All you can do is return to this breath,
witness this heirloom rose
unfurl from its tight-capped home.

The scent of the ancients stops you midstride.
The hummingbird comes from time to time,
tilting her head in just the right way,
sharing freely her worldly advice.

Pause, still, quiet,
nothing is more breathtaking than this moment.
So, this is what you can trust, this is how to pay it forward.
The rose, the hummingbird, the grief,
the being lost and found, the breaking ground.
The love.
Remembering.

The Maiden

"It takes discipline to be a free spirit."

Gabrielle Roth

Chapter 1

The Maiden

Reclaiming Creativity, Restoring Authenticity

Maiden, wild at heart, courageous spirit.
Your zest for life is infectious.
Your timeless touch lights up the world,
your song a symphony for authenticity.
Underworld adventurer, shadow dancer, tightrope walker.
Dream weaver, river explorer, mountain climber.
Wings unfurl as you launch your lifework into the world.
A visionary on a mission to reclaim lost hope and restore faith.
Your unforgettable song arouses the divine feminine to rise.
Heirloom seeds of right action, gathered and sewn across the lands.
Your essence inspires humanity to take the oath of service
to all sentient beings.
Original at the core, your soul matrix is born anew.
Share it freely with this wild world—
this is your Maiden's homecoming.

Who Is the Maiden?

The Maiden lives each day as an adventure. Her verve for life is infectious. Her innocence is pure. She is unapologetically passionate. She knows what she believes in, and she stands mountain strong in her personal values. The Maiden is wildly creative in her approach to life. Her perspective sees all angles.

The Maiden is an intuitive problem solver; resourcefulness is her key. She is unafraid of her own shadow. She knows the depth and wisdom that come from the darkness, for she has been there. She interrupts the trance of living blindly inside her own illusions, no longer skimming the surface of life; a wise innocence is embodied and integrated at her core. She can maneuver through all realms—shadow to light, innocence to strength, forgiveness to love. She feels good inside the quiet company of her own self. Authenticity is her superpower. Her approach to life is fueled by her optimism and a faith that has been earned through her commitment to living her best life.

The Maiden restores her energy daily with mental, physical, and spirited practices that keep her connected and devotional. Her body–mind channels are like liquid sunshine—she knows how to listen within and to feel her gut instincts. Her inner visions flow with depth and grace into her passion projects. She is courageous and understands the risks that need to be taken in order to fulfill her mission in life. An activist at heart, she follows the steady pulse of what she knows needs to be expressed in the world. She represses nothing. Her youthful and passionate verve for life imprints infinite empowerment—both creative and fearless—into the hearts and minds of all those she greets on her journey.

The Maiden's Voyage

Having more questions than answers is natural. The Maiden's journey is curious—exploratory, inquisitive, expansive. At the core, it's about understanding the difference between past and future narratives and true intuition. In their purest form, intuitive messages come without a back story. Intuition is not created from past or future projections. It comes from an impulse, a sensation in the body that says, "*Yes, this is how I feel, this is what I want, this is coming soon.*"

The maiden's voyage is about reclaiming our right to live with creativity while maintaining faith in our inner heroine. When we can remember our playful, unique, and devotional nature, we can call upon the maiden to guide us towards wholeness. One step along the path of restoring our inner maiden to her full expression is understanding when we spend too much energy pleasing other people. When we embrace new beginnings as a rite of passage rather than something to be dreaded or feared, we open another door towards freedom. When we understand how we block our ability to receive love, abundance, and success, we begin to unravel how our fears hold us back. We release roles, habits, and relationships that no longer serve us.

We know we are on the path. We become aware of how we may say one thing and feel another. When we get quiet enough to feel everything that we have been unwilling to feel, we receive permission to be our true self. We are invited to navigate the Maiden's voyage home towards creative living.

How can I create the right rhythm for myself in this stage of my life? What's currently brewing? What stokes my fire? How can I feed that fire to stay present inside my own evolution? As change is the one thing our ecosystem, humanity, the universe can rely on—how am I keeping up with the shifts in my own evolving consciousness? How is my Maiden shadow of people-pleasing running the show? What if I released my fear of new beginnings? What if I pursued the hobbies, projects, or skills that would enhance my sense of being and belonging on this planet?

It's never too late. Nothing is lost—every experience on your journey informs the next. Embrace each adventure as a creative pursuit. Restore hope, reclaim your inner guide, orient to the compass within; the Maiden voyage is ready to begin. Get expansive in your perspective. Let go of the martyr, the victim, the "*I am not enough*" mentality. You are not broken. When you recognize the shame-blame-guilt dance, you have the opportunity to wake up and reclaim the creative, joy-infused life you are meant to live. Give yourself permission to rebalance your system and deepen your capacity to experience joy, love, and wholeness.

When you commit to a daily dose of creativity, you connect with channels and pathways inside the body and in your external life. This deeper connection becomes a catalyst for reclaiming creative powers and restoring faith in your soul mission. Tend to your inner fires with steadiness and passion.

Dare to be you for you.
Dare to be a wildcard.
Dare to create free of the critics.
There is freedom within this process.
Your personal evolution deserves to be vast,
multidimensional, personal, unique.
Trust your liberation.

Tracking the Narrative

We are all born into this life with a pure essence that is uniquely our own. We inherit traits from our ancestors, and we build our own stories based on our life experiences. As children, we are like sponges; there is no doubt that we are deeply affected by the events of our younger years. If there was an excess of imbalanced emotions from our caregivers—anger, abuse, disconnection, abandonment, or addiction, for example,—we form survival strategies and coping mechanisms. Such unresolved trauma will have a direct impact on how we live as adults. That is why we must reveal the entire range of our life experience so we can more fully understand our imbalances and the stories we either tell ourselves or play out in our life.

Meditation

Take a moment right now. Close your eyes, place your hands on your heart, and listen. Invite in compassion. Take deep, full breaths. Scan your early childhood years.

What memories come forward?

Were there any attention-seeking behaviors or belittling strategies or experiences or struggles that relate to your current situation? Were there ways in which you gave your power and sense of self-worth away to accommodate others?

Can you get a sense of how the psyche develops repetitive behaviors based on your life story?

This is one of the greatest keys on the path towards personal liberation. When we reveal the complete narrative of our life's story, we understand more fully the impulses, patterns, and cycles inside our emotional, mental, physical, and spiritual bodies. We can then compassionately interrupt the limiting stories we continue to tell ourselves. With practice and compassion, we learn to catch ourselves playing out a narrative based on our past. Then we can begin anew.

When we discover the narrative inside the Maiden archetype, we can see more clearly why we hold ourselves back from tapping into our dreams, from attuning to our creativity and activating our full potential. As we weather the storms in life, we may disconnect from our essential nature. The true self gets shut down, and we begin to organize our life in a way that feels safe. While this reaction makes sense, it's like swimming upstream in a raging river.

If you have an unresolved, burning desire to change your life and reclaim a meaningful, creative, and embodied existence, and you don't act upon it, this blocked energy gets lodged in the body. This creates imbalance, eventually leading to lack of fulfillment, unhappiness, and disconnection from your greater sense of purpose. This can come through in the narrative of lost dreams. The story of *"It's too late to fulfill my dream life now"* takes a grip and steals energy, which results in unhappy relationships, excess stress, and inner disharmony.

If you feel you are too old to begin again, you are living inside the Maiden's shadow. The infectious zest and youthful spirit of the fully realized Maiden archetype is timeless. There is no age within the Maiden's wheelhouse.

The aging process is wildly profound, deeply nourishing, and wise beyond measure. When we radically and unconditionally accept ourselves—our changing bodies, our wisdom wrinkles, our softening bellies—we empower the creative shape-shifter within. Understanding where and why we find inner resistance or lack helps us transform the mainstream narratives of lost dreams, lost beauty, and lost youthfulness. We step into the direct experience of the Maiden's radiance through all stages and cycles of life.

It may be time to listen to how you speak to yourself daily about your body image. What negative core beliefs are stuck in your mind? It may be time to interrupt the trance you are in and begin dismantling the narrative of *"If only I did this,"* or *"I should have done this, and it's too late to begin again."*

When you interrupt the negative energies, you generate space to free yourself from personal and collective narratives of limitation. You regain faith, commit to creative practices, and welcome hope and optimism. You no longer give up. You grant yourself permission to begin anew every day. You enable yourself to change your mind, navigate a new direction, and reclaim inner vitality. A wildly authentic embodiment of the essential self emerges and radiates out into the world.

When you commit to your creative and soul-infused practices, you drop out of your complex mind patterns. Your ego softens, you feel more. Intuitive whispers spill like gems out of your mouth. You live not just out of practicality, logistics, schedules, materialism, success, wealth, and societal or familial acceptance—you follow your inner counsel. You liberate the repressed inner child, the lost Maiden waiting for her fairy tale dreams to come true. You lean into what lights you up rather than what brings you down. You learn to rest, to advocate for yourself, and to strengthen your boundaries. Your inner desires become your greatest allies—you do what you do because it must come out of you. The awakened Maiden is fearlessly creative in her life's quest.

What are you unwilling to feel?
Can you slow down enough to ponder?
Sketch, scribble, make sculptures in the sand.
Unearth the invisible, reveal it to the seen.

And when the heavy fog disperses inside the web
of the limitless sky—
move with courage into this honest meeting place.
Barefoot on steppingstones, in cold salty ocean.
Hold on to what matters most, feel every ounce of it.
Plunge with grace, walk your Maiden home.
Your heart—mind adventures into the lavish garden of your dreams.

Embody the Maiden Archetype

To embody the Maiden archetype is to reclaim creativity, gather courage, restore faith in your biggest dreams, and live with a lust for life that is unapologetically authentic. The Maiden's journey home into this creative and youthful paradigm begins with the daily embodiment of archetypal characteristics.

Meditation

Feel back into a time when you were fearless, wildly creative, and free—even if you only get a glimmer. What were the conditions in your life? What was your relationship with yourself, and with others? What lit you up?

Close your eyes and recall a time in your life when you felt invincible—ready to take on any task, climb any mountain, travel, explore, fall head over heels in love, fight for what you believe in, embrace the open road before you.

This is the Maiden's essence, and this lives inside you.

Can you get a sense of the energy inside the Maiden archetype? Notice what this evokes for you.

Change may be knocking on your door. This book has landed in your hands because now is the time to rekindle your dreams. They are not lost by you, not lost on you; they are still living within you. Now is the time to revision your vision and call your inner Maiden home.

Change is the one thing you can count on in life. The human mind, heart, and body are constantly changing. The earth, air, fire, water, and ethers are always transforming before you.

The Maiden's quest is to stay present within the shape-shifting roles, jobs, relationships, and challenges in life. This requires self-reflection, intention, and regulation. Holding your mind as a vessel of pure potential is the task of the Maiden. Weaving your prayers and dreams with clarity into the tapestry of your life is the mission.

Get crystal clear on the essence inside the seed of your prayers.
Align your body–mind–heart channels to merge with this vibration.
Build your daily existence around this energy.
What kind of alchemy does it hold?
Feed it with devotion, connect to your dreams.
Let go of controlling the outcome.
Know what you stand for and believe in it.
Cast your soul passions far and wide.
This is how dreams come alive.

Working with the Maiden's Shadow

Inside every living energy there is a shadow. As in day to night, sun to moon, the earth is made of opposing forces. Yet these forces generate dynamic energy, create change, and reveal all parts of the whole. When you can track the shadow inside your own being, you have the opportunity to understand the next phase of your healing journey. You uncover what may be unconsciously ruling your life and holding you back from staying true to your soul purpose.

If you are ruled by the Maiden's shadow, you will be confined inside the limitations of your own mind while putting everyone else first before you. The Maiden's shadow is ruled by naivety, resentment, people-pleasing, and fear of change. If you constantly sacrifice your own joy for others and often feel resentful, angry, unseen, unheard, and unsatisfied, you are living in the Maiden's shadow. If you fear new beginnings and resist change, the Maiden's shadow is nudging you.

To embrace the shadow inside the Maiden archetype, you must be living from your personal essence and present to both the joys and the challenges in life. The medicine inside the Maiden's shadow is to recognize your patterns of being the people pleaser, the good girl, or the one who is fearful of taking risks or making changes. The way you sacrifice your own joy for others or block your zest for this one precious life is another key aspect of this shadow. When these patterns rule your life, dreams get lost inside your mind, buried down in the underworld; this is the mentality that says *"I could have or should have but didn't."* Over time, you stop believing that you can change your life and live with creativity and passion. Ultimately, you no longer stand for the life you want; you lose hope and succumb to a life of mediocrity. And you are not happy inside a mediocre life.

You can shift from lack to abundance, burden to freedom, grief to joy, repression to passion, broken to healed. Echoes of sovereignty reverberate from the underworld to the cosmic night sky, encouraging you to walk upon this precious earth embracing the beauty of who you truly are.

It's time to liberate yourself and reclaim courage, creativity, and a sense of adventure. If naivety keeps you trapped inside people-pleasing, self-sacrificing, and fear-based decision-making, it's time to work with the Maiden's shadow. If you have a narrative of staying in relationships, careers, and inauthenticity because you fear change, the truth-telling, passionate Maiden is ready to reclaim your life.

No time is lost. Release the victim within—no regrets, guilt, shame, or blame. Let go of the martyr identity. Now is the time to embrace your inner radiance Trust that the world will be a better place when you cast your radiance far and wide.

Put yourself in precarious places, access the strength in your edges,
fall and get back up again, laugh, cry, see the beauty in all things,
and remember—your inner Maiden is your inner warrior.

The repeating stories of lost opportunities in the past or future will inevitably arise. When they do, you have another teacher on your doorstep. You need no longer fear falling or failing. Take the risks required to follow your journey home. Visualize your inner Maiden holding a warrior's sword. See her peaceful and strong, radical and free, courageous and radiant. Call upon her when the shadow takes over. Gather the Maiden's zest for life and grant yourself permission to say no, to say yes. Let it come from a place within—not from others.

Begin each day as a creative adventure. Commit to a daily practice that clears your mind of toxic residue. Welcome moments of stillness, silence, and space to reflect personally without distractions. Allow yourself to have strong and clear boundaries. Greet any lower vibrational energies, both internally and externally, with compassionate understanding—this does not have to be your personal alchemy. No longer get pulled down by what you can't control.

In this moment, pause, soften, take a full inhale,
and a full exhale, soften again.
It may be time to invite your Maiden home.

Steppingstones along the River

The inner Maiden senses the beginning of the trailhead. You fearlessly cross the stones across the rushing rivers; you navigate by your inner compass, following your gut instincts. You are not afraid of failure or falling. The underworld's darkest days and longest nights have brought you to a temple of resourcefulness and resilience. Pushing through past traumas and challenges you emerge from the dark night of the soul. After that initiation, the Maiden's flame is reborn, and you begin anew.

The Maiden's journey is like crossing a rugged, glacier-fed, raging river. In all seasons, cycles, and stages of life you trust that crossing the river happens one stone at a time. Each morning you ignite the candle within. Light lives inside the center of your body, where the earth channels meet the vastness of the sky within the human form, where the water meets the sandy shoreline, where the sun and moon dance from shadow to light. This is your Maiden's capacity. Your energy is wildly independent, infectious, awe-inspiring.

Your mind is the remedy. Understanding mental processes is the greatest teacher in your life. Freedom comes from being aware of the thoughts that rule your mind—the thoughts that cause you to fall into negative actions, words, and feelings over and over again.

If you do not steady yourself through intentional practices such as creativity and passion projects, the mind will sabotage the Maiden's zest for life. It will pull you back into a life of people-pleasing. It will stop you from launching into new beginnings. Fear of taking risks will hold you back from expressing your truth. It will keep you falsely safe inside a life of mediocrity and shallow living and loving. The Maiden's homecoming begins by tracking your shadows. Only then can you shift the ways you hold yourself back from living life to its fullest.

See yourself for who you are, not for who you are not.
This cosmic dance of life gets multidimensional
when you accept the invitation.
This is no part-time gig, show up for yourself every day.

Get quiet to hear the shadows inside your mind.
When they speak to you, know they are calling for your attention.
Pushing the imbalances away will only expand their grip on you.
Forgiveness is the path to remembering who you are.
Give yourself permission to begin again.
What you nourish in your life will flourish.

Persephone: The Maiden Who Rises from the Underworld

The mythological tale of the Greek goddess Persephone epitomizes the Maiden's shadow journey: she focuses on pleasing people around her; she lives a passive and anxious life. Against her will, she gets pulled down into the underworld, robbed of everything she once knew. She meets her own shadow and finally surrenders to the dark night of her soul as a rite of passage. Like the phoenix rising from the ashes, she awakens reborn as a wildly creative, deeply passionate and fearless goddess. After her adventures in the underworld, she embraces this precious life with a mythic wisdom and an unforgettable legacy, planting seeds of truth, beauty, and compassion everywhere she goes.

Persephone holds the key to soul retrieving, shadow dancing, creative wildfire, and timeless living and loving.

Persephone's Journey

Eager to please, waiting for her destiny to unfold, the once inno-cent Maiden falls into the underworld. Resistant, she fights her shadows. Fearful, lost, and alone, she no longer knows who she is or where she is going.

Gone are her naive hopes of being swept off her feet. "Suffering is a rite of passage," the wise elder whispers. "Take these seeds, swallow them whole. You will endure this trial; your inner power is coming now. Release everything and let your strength in."

The darkness penetrates her fully. She has no choice but to surrender her preconceived fantasies and fairytales. The alchemical fire burns wildly.

She awakens to witness her own cosmic rebirthing. Her once clouded vision is now crystal clear. With the death of her shadows, she is reborn into the skin of her soul house.

Welcome home, sweet one, you have endured the darkest of nights.
She hears her name in the distance—"Persephone, you are ready
to emerge whole, stronger, wiser than ever before."

Lightning strikes, thunder roars, the spring rains pour down.
And in a flash, she rises from the underworld, seeds
of compassion rooting from her magnetic light.
Resplendent gardens bloom all over the earth.

Creative Pursuits to Awaken Your Inner Maiden

Creativity can take many forms. If you were shut down as a child or adult and told you were not an artist, singer, dancer, writer, etc., it is now time to reclaim your creative warrior. You get to make the rules. You get to choose which direction, medium, and style to pursue.

What if you gave yourself one creative date per week where you dedicated some focused, uninterrupted time for you to get into the creative zone?

What if you committed to one small creative act daily?

You can go deeper into revealing your inner artist when you schedule this creative date in the same way you would any other appointment, work deadline, or date with a friend.

The results are profound when you ask for support and guidance from your intuition and the forces, guides, and teachers all around you. Creating in a natural environment—at the park, beach, by the water, in the forest, under the light of the moon—can be deeply healing. We can learn so much about our inner artist by basking in nature. Lean into the practices that light you up and bring you more alive. Observe the positive state you enter when you are fully embodied inside the practice. This is the channel of creativity. This is the Zen energy, where a sense of deep time fuels the passionate building energy of the Maiden.

Make art for the sake of art making.

Become an activist for what you know to be true.

Stay steady, awake, and aware inside your creative process.

Have a free-flow journal session, pick a daily oracle card, paint with watercolors, garden outside and inside, mend your clothes by hand, knit, crochet, make jewelry. Sing loud and proud. Meditate, have kitchen dance parties, make altars and offerings for the earth.

Be an activist for a cause you believe in, volunteer your time, take a stand for what you know to be true. Protest for a cause that pulls on your heart. Plan adventures that scare you. Travel to a country you have always wanted to visit.

You are the artist and the creator. Your ability to truly embody your visions and dreams is the key to realizing them.

Pay attention to those moments that stop you in your tracks. When a flash of lightning strikes in the form of an idea, clarity arrives. Creativity pours out of you and a force of faith and devotion becomes louder than the inner critic. Drop everything else, let time stand still, and immerse yourself in this alchemy.

I liberate myself from guilt, shame, and fear,
from the "could-should-would" complex.

I receive the gifts of my own creative, unique,
sensual, and sovereign radiance.

Tending my gardens, I paint wildly, and dance freely—
I do this for my own evolution.

My inner alchemist desires such affection.
I stand in my own sovereignty.

And when disbelief and separation occur, I know that this is
the sign to find the path once again. I trust that I am the one I
have been waiting for. Everything else is a bonus. I receive my
authentic genius, and let it flow out of me freely.

Practices for Embodying the Maiden

~

The Maiden's Voyage:
A Guided Visualization

Visualize yourself in a field of wildflowers. Observe the setting in a way that is crystal clear. What color, shape, size are the flowers? Are there any bees or other insects close by? What does the air feel like? Is the sun shining? Is there water close by? What does the landscape look like?

Begin to observe your breath, taking inhales and exhales for four to six counts. Visualize leaving your life behind you right now—the roles and responsibilities, the questions and concerns. Let them all go for now. This is a journey to reclaim your inner Maiden and release all limitations. What beliefs, thoughts, and ways of being are holding you back from your creative, authentic, and intuitive self?

Scan through your life, highlight what may be holding you back. Imagine laying each obstacle down, every weight of concern, each stone in your heart, all the ways in which you limit yourself—as if each story is a stone ready to be placed upon the earth. No longer are these energies needed. It's time to let them go. As you release these limiting beliefs and experiences, trust that they have brought you to where you are right now. All your experiences have led you to this place of awakening.

Set an intention now to reclaim your most creative self. What do you need to know in order to awaken the Maiden within? What will support you in reclaiming your zest for life? Listen for the words that want to come through your prayers. "I am living each day of my life inside my creative energy channels." Or "My life is an alive and creative pursuit to fulfill my dreams."

Come back to observing the wildflowers around you and the stones that you excavated out of your body. Are you ready for a journey to reclaim your wholeness?

Visualize a tunnel in the earth or imagine the root systems of large trees. See yourself now going on a journey through the underworld. As you move through the darkness of the underbelly of the world, find a path that allows you to go all the way down into the heart of the earth. Drink in the richness of the soil, let the nutrients replenish your energy body. Let your whole body be nourished by the earth's fertile alchemy.

Find a light, a door, or a bridge. Move towards that now and enter the portal of the underworld. Observe this whole new landscape before you. With your intentions and prayers, begin to create a sculpture that is symbolic of your dreams. Observe any symbols, shapes, colors that come through your creation. Now gather wood to build a ceremonial fire. Sit in front of the fire, and invite all your supporting and compassionate guides, teachers, and soul friends to join you. They will support you in reclaiming your wholeness.

Begin to track ways in which you block your creativity. All the times you have lost hope. The times of illusion, lost power, and attempts to fit in. The patterns of people-pleasing and sacrificing your own joy for the sake of others. Begin to give these ways of being, living, and believing to the fire. Clean your energy body of these vibrations. Is there anything else to clear out? Give it to the fire. Feel the support and encouragement from your guides and companions—they are cheering you on. Welcome any symbols, intuitive flashes, or affirmations that came through this journey. Give thanks for any insights that emerged.

Begin to make your way back home to the field of wildflowers. As you voyage home, feel the Maiden's creative genius awakened and integrated within you. Faith restored, creativity reclaimed, intuitive channels integrated.

Welcome home sweet one, the world awaits your true essence.

～

Clearing Negativity, Aligning with Beauty:
A Free-Write Practice

Set a timer for 10 minutes and free-write or journal the ways you negatively self-talk or complain, feel lack, feel burdened by others, or speak of others in a disparaging way. Get it all out.

Then free-write about the beauty you see in nature, in the world, in your family/community, and in yourself. Align with this high vibration and welcome it into your life.

Sit in silence for five minutes. With each inhalation breathe in the essence of beauty; with each exhale breathe out the essence of compassion.

Create and record three or more personal affirmations to inspire your mind when you go into lack or negativity.

For example:
"I am abundant." "I am passionate." "I am a timeless and limitless channel for inner beauty."

～

Ritualize Creative Acts

Before you begin any creative pursuit, have your journal ready.

Set a personal intention for your creative date: bring to your awareness at least three things that may be limiting, negative, or repetitive in your way of seeing, believing, or relating to your life.

Write them down, visualize them leaving your consciousness, or imagine throwing the limiting vibrations into a ceremonial fire—watch them burn and transform. Now, invite in three or more gratitudes, prayers, or visions for your life. Visualize them manifested; feed them with your positive vibrations.

Take time to connect with your breath, soften your whole body, light a candle, and welcome any signs, symbols, and messages from your intuition. Sense beyond into the spiritual, ancestral realms. If you have a specific question, you can connect with your ancestors, guides, and intuitive nature by addressing them from a meditative prayer state.

For example:
I am open to receiving support from the universe at this time.

Send me a sign and let me know that I am on the path towards living my best life.

The more you ask for support while connecting to creative and intuitive pursuits, the more information you will receive. This is a powerful daily practice of simultaneously listening, receiving, and giving.

Honor the creative process from a place of freedom and intention.

Sparkles of sunlight on the water's surface.
The trees will listen, hug them often.
The roses will sing love songs while the moon whispers,
"Breathe deep, feel everything,
shape-shifting is your higher power."

~

Self-Reflection Practice

Take five minutes or more to sit in silence. Connect to your breath. Close your eyes and bring your focus inwards. Place your hands over your heart and feel its rhythm. Let go of the past and the agenda for the future.

Visualize a flame in the center of your body, let it rise to your heart, and sink down into the earth. Listen within and ask yourself, *"What wants to come through my creative practice today?"*

Feel for the first impulse. It may be a color, image, symbol, sound, scent, or words.

Open your eyes and journal about your experience.

Fill in the blanks to fuel your creative energy following the self-reflection practice:

I am _____

I will _____

I create _____

I believe _____

I choose _____

I share _____

I desire _____

I release _____

I connect _____

I am _____

I will _____

Step inside your own being,
unravel to remember who you are.
Receive guidance from higher powers,
trust that you are supported.
Tend to the fertile garden of your dream channels.
In return your body-intuitive response
will grow the most exquisite flowers.

Journal Prompts to Integrate the Maiden Within

The Embodied Maiden's Characteristics
Creative | Authentic | Passionate | Optimistic
Courageous | Intuitive | Risk Taker

What aspects of the Maiden archetype would you choose to embody more fully?

What qualities do you feel are living strong within you?

Create a personal affirmation to inspire the Maiden to come alive fully; let it be a creative expression.

For example:

I am a conduit for truth, radiance, and creativity.

I actively release the thoughts, words, and actions that come from inherited negativity.

I am fluid, calm, wild, cosmic, and fearless.

I free myself from the worldly weights that cloud my life's mission.

Every day, I commit to sacred practices that align, awaken, and ground me into my authentic presence.

Journal Prompts to Work with the Maiden's Shadow

Characteristics of the Maiden's Shadow
Afraid of Change | Eager to Please People | Resentful
Angry | Naive | Self-Sacrificing

What aspects of the Maiden's shadow do you identify with?

How could you be contributing to these limitations?

Where in your life does the shadow inside the Maiden hold you back from your creative, authentic, and passionate self?

Where did you learn this behavior?

Why do you do it?

Create an affirmation for personal clarity to generate a shift in your consciousness and in your behavior moving forward, for example:

I people-please in my relationships because this is how I learned to receive love and attention as a child. Now I am ready to release this pattern and transform it into conscious giving and receiving based on unconditional truth and love. There are no more "shoulds" or "strings attached."

Write a short affirmation that you can use to re-route your habitual patterns of putting others' needs before yours, or when fear, anger, or grief begins to rule your life:

I will speak my truth when it arises. I know I have a right to live out my passions and embody unconditional joy and love. I no longer put everyone's needs before mine. I do this without feeling guilty, but with compassion, calm, and courage. Authentic living and loving are my journey home.

Love Notes to My Younger Self

Believe in the inner voice that says no.
Do not fear you will disappoint, miss out, or lose the game.
Let your yes come from your inner heroine.
Trust your gut, believe the flashes of insight
that strike your body like lightning bolts.

There will always be the waves of high to low.
Perfection is overrated.
How can you navigate the inner-to-outer
journey of this rugged terrain?
Stay true to what you believe is good and right.
Exercise the letting-go muscles.
Energy flows; tomorrow will be different.

Understand the law of not taking things personally.
Everyone has suitcases of stories and pain, it's not yours to carry.
Fearless living and loving are a daily ritual.
When you forget, practice forgiveness.
Lie upon the earth and gaze at the stars
to understand yourself more fully.
Rest when your body calls.

Take risks born from authenticity,
step out of the societal pressure cooker.
But your love—for you, for humanity, for the earth, the water,
the air, sun, and moon—will always land you home.
Trust the power of your visions.
This wondrous life beckons your heart to feel it all,
to move mountains so that all that is meant to come to birth and
grow, will thrive through you and around you.
Be the faith carrier, the heart-led,
spirit-infused visionary of your dreams.
This precious earth is ready to receive your gifts.

The Mother

*"It's not about how much you do,
but how much love you put into what you do that counts."*

Mother Teresa

Chapter 2

The Mother

Foraging Love to Fortify Spirit

Now is the time to step inside the womb of a love source
that casts out into the world—further than imagined,
deeper than words can hold,
more potent than the heart has felt before.

And when your blood surges hot,
your skin tingles with the taste of salty tears
upon your quivering lip,
and the monarch's wing flutters within—
trust that you will be midwifed inside this healing force.

This is your creation story in the making;
this is you birthing your spirit alive.
This is you mothering self in a way that is nectar for your soul.

Allow the softness of your gaze to widen your lens.
Feel the cells in your body rekindle the ancient ones above,
merge with the bounty of the earth's alchemy below.

Glimmers of your wildest creations spark alive.
Anchored, abundant, and fertile,
your own nurturing capacity now dialed to its brightest frequency.

This ancient soul of the mother holds the power to heal the world.

Evolving the Essential Mother in You

The Mother is the life force inside all acts of creation. Mother Earth with her impeccable creations is the epitome of this archetypal force and source. The Mother can discern, plant, and nurture her visions, intentions, and prayers deep in the dark soil while patiently awaiting their full expression of growth and manifestation. The awakened Mother within is tethered to the workings of compassion, anchored to the earth on which she creates, and resourceful beyond measure. The evolved feminine frequency within the Mother archetype holds the wisdom to see the larger picture while tending to the pressing details inside the sequential order that exists in all living things. The Mother knows how to make something from nothing. Her intuitive capacity understands that new life sparks from darkness. The cycles of birth, death and rebirth are held within her matrix. The Mother knows when to let go, what to weed out of the garden, and acts through honest inner body listening into outer body expression.

The Mother archetype is vast and can take many forms. She may grow babies in her womb for nine months and tirelessly raise her children in the world. Or she may birth soul projects, raise animals, or pour creative energy into her life's calling. The Mother archetype must maintain a steady flame throughout a lifetime, whether raising a cause, or a family.

Steadiness and the capacity to nurture is her superpower.

Recalibrating beliefs, attitudes, and daily systems to align with the embodiment of this essential feminine way is the path towards healing self while expressing this frequency of healing in the world.

The Mother knows that her body is her temple. Although society expects her to act or look a certain way, she knows how to nourish herself. She understands how to shed toxic thought patterns and transform them into resilient compassion and timeless wisdom that acknowledges the goodness in all things. She celebrates her curves, life stories, wrinkles and the stages of her menstrual cycle. The Mother within understands the struggles of her ancestors and all women who have birthed humans, creations, visions, and wisdom into this world. When she is overwhelmed by fatigue, fear and the weight of the world on her shoulders, she lays her body upon Mother Earth's womb to replenish her vitality.

The embodied Mother greets her masculine spark to enhance her feminine frequency. Embracing her inner child, she discovers the world with an awakened vision, choosing love over comparison, acceptance over judgement. She pulses with a genuine desire to enhance the quality of life for humanity and all living beings. She is a well of deep compassion who knows how to nurture her spirit while simultaneously nourishing others. She emanates deep grace, fierce love, an inner power that senses danger in any given moment. Like a lioness protecting her young, she can tap into the darkness of injustice from miles away and will do anything to gather her family to keep them safe.

The Mother knows how to prepare a feast for her soul family. Her warm hugs heal. She listens with a penetrating presence that makes you feel valued and worthy. She has your back; she believes wholeheartedly in you. This is the embodied Mother.

Reclaiming the inner Mother means listening in order to feel, while remaining fluid to grow. Trusting when to let go and when to engage, on both a practical and intuitive level. The inner Mother creates a life with less complexity and more clarity, while tending the hearth of the earth for the generations to come.

Mothering to Unearth Creative Potential

We all have a narrative around mothers, whether it's our relationship with our own mother, how we mother ourselves, or nurture our creativity, career, or soul's calling. Or perhaps we are mother to children, pets, or the special beings in life.

How we have been cared for is a formative experience that we can all relate to as human beings. We are born into this world in complete vulnerability. Our existence and survival as newborns is made possible by our caretakers. The imprint of our earliest years affects the rest of our life, whether we are conscious of this or not.

We are sponges to our mother's, father's, and caretaker's energy. We all have a story that exists inside the Mother archetype, be it positive or negative. Hence, when we begin to unpack our childhood, there is no shortage of good work to be done as we discover how we nurture our own lives, let alone the lives of others.

To embody the Mother archetype in physical, emotional, intellectual, and spiritual ways begins by taking care of the full range of our personal experiences—from the deepest wounds to the greatest gifts. Mothering of self goes far beyond mothering of children, and it means reprogramming how we care for ourselves. Reshaping the narrative around how we mother "Self" requires an investigation into how we show up for ourselves daily. On a physical level, can we honor our bodies as sacred, feed ourselves appropriately, and fall in love with our physical form? Can we tend to our emotions as messengers who direct us to the necessary inner work? Can we still the mind long enough to sift through the toxic patterning and realize when and where the mental narrative needs to shift? Lastly, can we tend to our speaking words—whether our inner chatter or spoken out loud to other people—so that they elevate the listener?

All these parts of us are a work in progress. Think of them as their own gardens, each one needing to be tended—planted, weeded, watered, and harvested. Each day we have an opportunity to let go of harmful patterns and let in expansive grace. This way we align all our personal channels into a deeper sense of nurtured wholeness. Our creative potential becomes unearthed. We arrive at our dynamic, fertile, and wildly abundant nature, ready to express its beauty in the world.

Be an expander of positive life force energy.
Mother yourself in the name of radical love.
What you feed grows.
The more you come home to your true nature,
the higher the frequency of love you generate.
Naturally your mind and body
will synchronize with the soul work
you are destined to do on this earth.

Nurturing as a Path of Expansion and Love

The initiatory path of the Mother is in how we tend to our daily needs, how we say yes or no, how we choose to let go and then let in the energy of nurture. The Mother archetype comes alive within when we witness our truth, know and trust what we feel most compelled to stand for. Mothering of self is a fluid practice of expansion and contraction to maintain balanced energy inside the weave of our daily lives. To look deeply into how we deny ourselves nourishment, love, happiness, and joy is to recognize how we block ourselves from embodying our true self.

As a vulnerable young child, we were deeply influenced by our caregivers, mothers and fathers. We did what we could to please them, to adore them, to reject them. We did our best. We may have loved them, despised them, or rebelled completely against them. We all come with stories and memories around mothering.

Here is the deeper calling:
How can you best mother yourself at this time
in order to create, expand, and cultivate the life you want?

Now the work is to put yourself first. You are worthy of this care. Getting clear on what you want and what you don't want is essential for building healthy boundaries. Making nourishing choices requires refining what you say yes to and what you say no to. This is an ongoing process. No longer wait for fatigue or hardship to spin you off balance. Rather, welcome in the mothering of self as an essential service to feed your highest self. Recalibrate with the delicate, exquisite, and fierce energy of Mother Earth herself to rekindle your wild power. You can create your reality. You are an expander of creation—of life to death to rebirth. Again, and again. This is your essential rhythmic power. And when you feel lack, fear, and unworthiness, lay your body down upon Mother Earth and feel her hold you, heal you, and rock you back into your true nature.

~

Recalibrating with the Mother's Source:
A Meditation

Let us begin here. Get soft in your body, let go of all your responsibilities, roles, fears, and stressors in this moment. Observe any tension in your body and take a deep sigh, followed by a long breath in. Connect to a landscape that you love – lush, abundant, collaborative, and expansive. Open your awareness to how deep the nourishment inside the earth runs—the fertile soil, the interconnected root systems from the trees, the microbes inside the soil that once came from fallen stars. Imagine this energy within you, ready to be accessed in a flash when needed.

Into the Womb Zone

The dark waters of the mother's womb are the first landscape we inhabit. This is true also for our mother's mother, her grandmother, her great grandmother, and great-great grandmother. The original landscape in which our creation story began through our mother's body, connected by the umbilical cord to keep us alive. The imprint of our mother's life journey lives within us.

If there was trauma during our mother's life or her mother's life, we may have inherited this blueprint whether we realize it or not. Included in this energetic mothering exchange is also deep love, radical joy, and ancestral wisdom. We can tap into this and begin the journey to empower our mother line. We can access a deep strength when we unearth our matriarchal lineage and hold our ancestors in both the healing states and the inherited gifts. We can then liberate ourselves and move into this lifetime weaving our own story, no longer carrying the weight of ancestral trauma.

You are a thread with which your ancestral tapestry weaves itself. Wherever your family has come from and whatever it has gone through, your soul purpose is calling to you now. Now is the time to understand how learned behaviors, inherited belief systems, or societal structures may be ruling your life in ways that are destructive. If your mother or caregiver stayed in an abusive relationship and she did this for her family to stay together, you may have learned to normalize your own unhappiness for the sake of others. You may have inherited a patriarchal paradigm that keeps you living in guilt, shame, lack, or fear of your own success. This then acts like a chain reaction and reinforces the belief systems that keep you living in a field of unworthiness, further detaching from your full potential and purpose.

It is time to bring forward and name these energies, in order to detach them from your body. Through this process of forgiveness and understanding you can heal your ancestral line. Begin by reclaiming the archetype of your inner Mother—embodied, abundant, grounded, supported and supportive, creative, fertile, vast, wise, nurturing.

Practice being over doing.
Practice compassion over judgement.
Work with fear and resistance as a way
into a deeper understanding.
Your body begs you to open the temple door into this shifting
realm of the human experience.
Practice sitting with discomfort over numbing it.
You are equipped with the tools to push through
the fear-guilt-shame complex
into resilient grace and fierce love.

Healing the Mother Wound: Breaking Old Cycles, Amplifying Goodness

Many indigenous cultures believe that our actions will affect seven generations to come and heal seven generations back. According to those ancient teachings, you can do the work of healing so that you become a good ancestor and no longer pass along the trauma of the past. By honoring your ancestors for all they endured and understanding that they did the best they could in the conditions and consciousness they lived in, you become a front-line ancestral healer.

You may feel called to do the work of forgiveness, shifting the conditioned beliefs, transforming the narrative for yourself. Thus, you pass positive change and wellness along to your families, friends, communities, and to Mother Earth. Family trauma can slide and sift through your subconscious and rule parts of your life, without you realizing it. The untold stories, unfinished business, unspoken or silenced family agreements become the inner abuser if you do not resolve them through your body, mind, and lifestyle. It is up to you to name, detach, forgive, and reclaim the way you choose to nurture yourself in this lifetime. If you do not do this work, bitterness creeps in, resentment builds, repressed emotions get pushed down further. This results in an unfulfilled, imbalanced energy that can lead to physical, mental, or emotional illness.

The saying "may you leave no stone unturned" points to the work of healing the ancestral tapestry. Knowing which inner flame to ignite and which fires no longer need to get lit is perhaps the best work of your life. In any given situation, relating to your relationship with the earth, and to your own mothering of self or others, ask yourself this one question:

"What is the best goodness here?"

This simple yet expansive question will connect you to the present moment. It will light the torch of goodness over inherited belief systems. It will allow you to connect to your own truth and enhance the frequency of compassion, right action and love. Take that simple sentence "What is the best goodness here?" and put it inside your heart. Ground this energy of goodness into the earth and feel it inhabit your spine, to be remembered even in the toughest moments of conflict and pain.

This work takes courage. We must discern what is driving the goodness: is it unresolved guilt or is it the pure essence of goodness?

This is essential for cleaning and clearing our energy field—not only for our own inner Mother to thrive, but also to tend to the climate crisis that humanity has caused on Mother Earth's body. It is the call of our times to be in a paralleled state of advocacy and healing for the earth and for how we take care of ourselves. This requires honesty over denial, recalibration over destruction, and foundational healing over chasing the status quo.

If we can break the ancestral programming that we know needs to be destroyed, those who come after us will have a different foundation in which to grow and thrive. When we do the conscious work of releasing old ways, it can feel like we are waking up from a slumbered state. The clouded mind, armoured heart, and weighted body can feel liberated. This can happen quite quickly when we give ourselves permission to do so. This leads into the creation of fertile and nurtured soil from which we can plant our vision seeds for this lifetime. Our DNA recalibrates and attunes to a higher vibration of purpose, joy, and freedom to mother all parts of who we are, past, present and future.

Like a seedling bursting through
the mountain peak crevice to find the sun,
trust in the divine design of precarious places
and life-giving spaces.
Discover your edges, name your boundaries.
Do not fear your shadow—go there.

When you fall, gather yourself once again.
Live in wonder, see through the eyes of a child.
Laugh, cry, and let the wail of the trees
bring you to your knees.
See the beauty in all things.

And when you forget, remember that your
devotion to grace becomes your ability
to tap into the roots of love in any situation.

Mother Fatigue: When the Shadow Calls

When it is imbalanced, the Mother life force is shadowed by co-dependency, by the inability to receive, or by over-giving. Your energy becomes depleted, and resentment and judgement rule your existence. When you are tired, unfulfilled, and resentful you lose the connection to your essential self. When you are overly independent, your vitality gets drained. When you play the role of the victim or the martyr in order to receive acknowledgement, you disengage from your full potential. And when the shadow of shaming your body holds you back from loving yourself unconditionally, you block the light and beauty within.

The Mother's narrative can easily be overwhelmed by all the details it takes to birth and care for life's creations. The old saying "a mother's work is never done" may have been passed down to you through the lived experience of your ancestry. You can begin to examine this blueprint and remember that many hands make light work. You can shift the narrative from doing it alone, to asking for support and working collaboratively. When you give yourself permission to release control of every detail and outcome, you naturally see more clearly and act more intuitively.

When the Mother shadow narratives play out, as they will and they do at various times in life, it's your cue to summon the powers of the earth—Gaia, also known as the Earth Goddess. Adore every ounce of your body temple and honor all your efforts. The work is to shift the perception around lack and unworthiness in order to generate abundance and truthful acceptance of self. You may recognize these narratives in yourself, or your mother, your mother-in-law, your sisters, your partner or your friends. Once you see these patterns and how they take over, you see the path of healing opening before you. Spending time alone, going on a wellness retreat, saying no to extra work, reconnecting to your physical practices, getting enough rest, cooking nourishing food, adorning your body as your temple, receiving loving and supportive pleasure in any form—all will harmonize the Mother weave into a place of reciprocity.

Learning to honor your body as a sacred vessel is the work of birthing the inner mother alive. Once the cycles of lack, unworthiness, and fear are dismantled, the matriarchal line has space to evolve. Ancestral healing is soul love for both the human condition and the state of the earth. Can you listen to Mother Earth's call? She is asking us to wake up and make choices that are generative—personally and collectively. Plant your vision seeds with care, take only what you need, give back where you can. These seeds of potential will need watering, weeding, and true presence to weather the storms in life.

My Body, My Temple: A Journey of Radical Honoring

The way we perceive, accept or reject, and connect with our bodies may be the most cathartic work towards embodying the Mother archetype. In a media-driven culture the image of the perfect woman gets put in a box defined by her physical beauty over her intellect. These mind–body associations and comparisons project both darkness and light into our minds. We learn from a young age how to compare our bodies with the image of the "perfect" woman—thin, curvy, giving, caretaking, seductive. Our thoughts then begin to form about what we want to be like, what we don't want to look like; we live in a world of comparison versus authenticity.

It is possible to shift the focus from how we look to how we feel. Herein lies the deep and profound healing of our times. How can we mother our body with a wild acceptance, a radical nurturance, and an unlimited source of love? How can we honor our body as a place of worship? As we age, naturally our bodies change. If we view our changing bodies with constant judgement, comparison, and the desire to fit in, the vibration of lack will cause more stress and disconnection.

In addition, if there is unresolved childhood trauma such as sexual abuse, or physical or emotional violence, it may result in dissociation from the body that leads to disordered eating—either overeating to soothe or under-eating to control. We may turn away from nourishing our physical bodies, by ignoring our own needs, repressing our emotions, or neglecting self-care.

Shame is an emotion that begins in the body. It's viscerally seizing and debilitating; it stops you in your tracks. As children we experience shame when we are either disciplined or criticized by our parents, teachers, or peers. Perhaps we are innocently exploring our world, trying out cause and effect, and then we are reprimanded in a way that feels shameful. The feelings of shame imprint into our cells, get locked in the body. These shaming experiences become memories, which form narratives and relational patterns that we carry through our lifetime. We learn to block our creativity in fear of being judged. We mask our authentic nature in fear of judgement. Being shamed for our external appearance has a lasting imprint on how we live the rest of our lives. Often as children these experiences mark us, and we form habits and coping strategies to hide the shame, to push it down, to pretend it doesn't exist.

Trust and love are the antidotes to shame and fear. If there is trust, we feel freer to share the shame. If there is love and no judgement, we can soften our grip on fear and allow ourselves to be vulnerable. When we mother ourselves with love and trust, we can trace the trauma of childhood. We discover why we experience shame, guilt, fear, the need to hide, or the desire to seek attention and praise.

Mothering self requires honest listening and present awareness. The healing calls us closer to our inner child, to nourish and nurture her until she can rest deeply. When we feel safe and rejuvenated, we can tend to old wounds and unravel old stories until they no longer define us.

Meditation

In this moment, take a deep breath in, and a deep breath out. Place one hand on your heart, and one hand on your center. Give thanks for your body and for all it allows you to do daily. Merge your awareness with that of the earth's power and beauty. Touch down and tap into Gaia's fertile, abundant, and wildly creative force. See it in you, feel it support you. You are of this Gaia source, take this potent love frequency in and let it nourish and renew your body.

Picture a giant web before you. At the web's center is you as a newborn. Each bridge of the web's weave represents your personal history. Every relationship, adventure, and cycle creates the overall web of who you are. Imagine untangling the stories of abandonment, disconnection, and fear to generate space for the weave of personal authenticity and evolution. The healing in this present moment is powerful, and liberating. Take the seat of the Mother within. Walk hand in hand with Gaia's infinite abundance. Magnify your essential gifts out into the world, no longer hold back. No longer are you too much or too little. No longer fear failure or rejection.

Now you are ready to birth your visions alive.

Transform the Victim/Martyr Narrative: Free the Creative Channels

The shadows of the victim and martyr have for centuries been associated with the caregivers of the sick, the service providers, and the ones who raise the children and tend to the homestead. To recognize when you are playing a victim in your life is the path of true self-discovery. To name when martyrdom is woven into your identity is the call to embody the power in the Mother archetype.

The victim mentality is associated with constant complaining yet refusing to accept help. The victim's story exudes hardship and struggle, and this becomes her daily reality. The victim's identity is often built around stories like this: *I am always the one doing all the work, no one appreciates me, I never receive anything, I never have any help, my life is destined for failure.* She is enabled to keep living this way by receiving validation and support from others to continue to do so. She surrounds herself with company who reinforce her beliefs.

The victim gets defensive when challenged and seeks the struggle of *victimhood* to reinforce her own narrative.

The martyr paradigm differs in that it is ruled by the desire to forgo personal needs in order to tend to the needs of others. The martyr dismisses her own happiness, sacrifices her own desires in life. She does not ask for help, neither does she accept support when it is offered. She pushes others away to reinforce her identity as the doer, the taskmaster, the one who holds every detail and vision for others. Martyrdom may have an internal dialogue that sounds like this:

"I can't go for a workout, everyone else needs me right now. How can I leave this career for the job of my dreams when everyone here needs me? I must say no to this opportunity and sacrifice my own joy, staying in this unhappy, abusive, and toxic relationship, so I don't hurt others."

How to Transform the Martyr/Victim Paradigm

- Let go of identifying with the victim/martyr story
- Release the desire to control everything
- Ask for help and receive it when it is offered
- Interrupt the pattern of doing everything
- Mirror the martyr/victim in you by having an internal dialogue: "I hear you—you are always doing the work. I see you—you are always doing everything."
- Validate yourself and then ask, "What am I grateful for in this moment, how have I taken care of my own needs today? Is there a creative pursuit or self-care ritual that I can make happen today?"

The heart's work inside the service of mothering is to discern the true motivation behind each task, project, and action. The wisdom mother fills her own cup first, understands that self-care is essential to her ability to give back, asks for support, and is unconditionally compassionate. She understands where to place her time and energy, how to get the work done efficiently, and how to receive back through her own Gaia nature. When resentment and anger build and fatigue and stress become the rulers, she is able to pause, let go, and return to her own creative pursuits to replenish her temple.

To mother thy self is a great body of work. Tending the hearth
of the heart, ensuring nourishment is provided, rhythms are
followed, prayers are created, memories are collected, stars caught,
seeds planted, hardships endured, and challenges overcome.
Seedling to old growth, sun to moon, sea to shore, wolf to pup,
mother to child, you to you. This is me, mothering myself awake
with the magic and the mystery that makes this earth stir awake.

Embrace Your Inner Child: Heal to Reveal Your True Nature

Some of your childhood experiences may be either consciously or unconsciously holding you back from living a joyous, peaceful, and fulfilling existence. Bringing them to the surface will ultimately allow you to go deeper into every aspect of your life. To look at the things that may be repetitive patterns, habits, or blockages in your adult life is to uncover your inner child narrative.

As you begin to understand the origins of your desires, motivations, and habitual patterns, you get to see the bigger picture of who you are. Perhaps you understand your relationships, career choices, and personal complexities with greater compassion. You can welcome your longings and desires and begin to feed them with more love. You can liberate yourself from perfectionism, over-achieving, and unworthiness. This is deep healing work and always in progress. It takes forgiveness, compassion, and patience.

As humans we all carry secrets. We all have stories from our child-hood and direct experiences with toxicity, negativity, and shame. The important thing is to stay awake and aware when the inner child calls for support. She can come through the most unlikely of times to either sabotage and react or remind you of your light and joy. When you commit to practices such as journaling, meditation, visualization, movement, and creative pursuits, your inner child has a greater chance of speaking to you and leading you to healing and wholeness. You may have an opportunity in the moment to connect to a memory, unresolved feelings, and mind patterns to understand where the next cycle of healing work may need to go. Like the layers of an onion, the peeling is a process—sometimes uncomfortable, other times fast and peaceful.

Acknowledging your inner child by honoring every step of her journey is to embrace your wholeness and present-moment readiness to reclaim your ability to mother all aspects of your life: your home, your career, your creative and adventurous self. You're hungry to learn more, you thirst to dive deeper into relationships, and you nurture yourself deeply through all the portals.

Discover the ways in which you embrace your inner child, your past mothering efforts, your own mother's efforts—all in the name of self-liberation to create the existence you desire in this lifetime. This is the Mother in you, alive, connected, balanced and thriving. This is the child in you, playful, joyous, and wildly creative.

Ways to Connect to Your Inner Child

- Establish a connection by writing a letter to your child self with the intention to honor, nourish and heal the wounds of the past.
- Gather images of you as a child, and study them with curiosity.
- Begin a daily wonder/creativity journal; every morning state three or more ways you can approach your life with wonder and creativity.
- Engage in free-form, process-oriented creative pursuits such as painting, free dancing, journaling, visualization, and meditation.
- Remember/rekindle what you loved to do as a child—is there a way to bring this back into your life?
- Practice kindness towards yourself. When you get triggered into a state of overwhelming emotions—low self-esteem, anger, grief,

shame, abandonment, or lack—say to yourself: "I am here for you, I am sorry, I love you, I see you, I hear you."
- Create a positive affirmation to set your inner child free: "I am worthy of love, it is safe for me to play, I am a channel of wonder and joy."

Meditation

Open your visual field in this moment and picture a time in your childhood where you felt free, joyous, and safe. Remember what you loved and valued most. Now bring to the surface what you longed for, or what made you feel alone or disconnected. Imagine yourself in a natural setting that is kindred to you.

Visualize your adult self—holding the hand of your child self. You are standing together inside the center of a large labyrinth all around you. As you walk the outwards spiral, honor the longings and the loves, the disconnections, and the moments of pain by placing them as sacred relics upon the earth. Trust the open path forward, observe what you see and how you feel.

This becomes the living ceremony of your inner Gaia alive and well. Your energy field clears past pain as you trust the open path of love and renewal before you.

The Gaia Connection:
Ignite Life Force, Honor Abundance

In Greek mythology the earth was personified by the primordial goddess Gaia. Her elemental power is earth. Gaia was born out of chaos and gathered all the elemental forces to create the earth in all its beauty. Gaia's matrix as Mother of the earth is symbolic of fertility, agriculture, motherhood, renewal and rebirth, and environmental consciousness. This quintessential earth goddess has transcended time and become a contemporary symbol of our planet.

Gaia continues to ask us to take action to repair the environmental damage we have inflicted upon her. Time is of the essence; reshaping our attitudes and redirecting our actions away from the material towards a reciprocal lifestyle with the earth is critical. This means a shift away from consumerist ownership to earth stewardship. When we connect with Gaia's abundantly potent persona, physically and spiritually, we activate our own life force. We can connect with her infinite source to be an earth advocate and a good ancestor. By creating and sustaining life in all forms we fulfill our life's dreams.

The earth nurtures our physical bodies with the food that is grown, captivates our visual field with her exquisite beauty, and fuels our sense of wonder as we experience the ephemerality of her unpredictable nature. We tap into something deeper than the mundane of everyday life. The Earth Mother's force and current fragility reminds us to be humble, respectful, reciprocal, honoring her fertile temple.

*As we wake each morning and land our feet upon the earth,
may we remember to express our deepest gratitude for Gaia, and
recall that our survival is based on her existence, and her survival
is based on our actions. May we answer the call to be stewards of
the earth and good ancestors for all those coming after us.*

The earth is in a constant state of birth and death, the two largest events of our lifetime. Gaia teaches us how to nurture ourselves and others through the portal of birth and death, how we create our reality, how we choose to let go, set boundaries, and allow old parts of us to die away. We experience the deep well of grief when our beloveds cross over from the earth plane. We are held in the embrace of pure bliss when we experience the birth of new life on this earth. We experience loss through illness, be it physical or mental. We may fall deep into inertia, and then receive transformative mothering energy to be reborn once again. We learn that where there is light, there is shadow. Where there is new life, there is also death. Where there is pain, there exists love. We can see it in the cycles of the earth, the animals, and within our own existence.

When we train our inner rhythms to align with this knowledge of Gaia's cycles, we are naturally supported by her power and sustenance. We are more inclined to trust that we will be supported if we can allow ourselves to be a work in progress. When we fall, we can allow ourselves to fall, to rest, to receive support and rise once again. There is re-creation, re-invention, re-activation, and remembering within our own Gaia energy.

Perspective: Old Self Dying, New Self Emerging

In autumn as the days shorten, leaves surge their last energy into striking colors, trees send nourishment into their roots, temperatures lower, animals change their behavior. How can they resist or deny this evolution? The cycle is clear, the signs are non-negotiable. Survival depends on one cycle ending while another one begins.

Can we honor a similar journey in relationship to our inner Gaia frequency? When a habitual way of being, feeling, or thinking has lived out its time, can we stay awake, can we let go to create space for a new energy to emerge?

Our familiar patterns—whether shame or anger of the inner child, disconnecting from our bodies, or how we over-compensate, over-control, or deny ourselves nourishment and love—these are the clues and cues that direct us to heal and enhance the quality of our life.

~

Meditation

Open to the awareness that you are the witness to the toxic or negative patterns in your life. They do not define you any longer; catch them in the moment and allow them to die out of you. This is how we can nurture our inner Mother to blossom through all stages of life, with a sacred yet practical, fiercely loving, wildly forgiving, and deeply compassionate energy.

Every time we show up with heart intention,
a healing takes place.
Be it subtle or strong,
our past and future projections fall away.
An insight, a prayer, a sun-kissed ocean glimmer
returns us to wholeness.
We emerge with an expanded mind,
a recalibrated energy body,
and a renewed faith to keep doing the work that matters.

Your Epic Love Story

Build your daily existence around tending the flame of your inner temple. Greet your mind with resilient compassion, your heart with unshakeable grace, and your body with an abundant devotion that births new creations. Land home, anchor your roots, tread lightly upon the earth as you dance with the infinite nature of your own potential.

Begin with yourself—you matter—your words, thoughts, and actions matter. Listen, reach, support, soothe, receive, and give yourself fully to this path of kindness. Touch your loved ones with this living frequency of steady compassion. Joy becomes embodied when you give yourself permission to feel it.

Your inner matriarch is ready to cast her vision far and wide. This is the deepest level of soul work to be done on this planet at this time. There is goodness built inside the present moment, free of attachments, conditions, and rules. Align with your own sovereignty and willingness to flow with all aspects of life. There is no right or wrong, no good or bad—there is you liberating yourself from your own limiting beliefs, suffering, and destructive words and actions.

Step into the realm of a wild, unwavering, and deep self-love. It is right here waiting for you. Once you fall in love with yourself, the path opens to an infinite source of pure consciousness. This timeless frequency of love will land inside of you like the celestial holy matriarch herself.

You get to be a channel for this epic love story in this lifetime.

Trust that you are supported by the web of the past, present, and future. Even through life's fragmented past—the landslides, the deep dives, the exhausted and exalted experiences—you are embraced by a whole feminine divinity that goes beyond interpretation.

Every morning, revel in the tender touch of hand to heart, embrace the wondrous gift of your breath. Let the early dawn serenade of the bird's song become the symphony that dances your day awake. Light a candle to merge with the light forces around you and sit quietly inside the darkness of your own alchemy. No longer fear being alone. Be still long enough to hear the shadows in your mind, and the surges of joy in your center. This is a call to feel it all and to become the Mother source of your life's journey. You will know when and how to unearth the buried treasures waiting for you. The temple of your epic love story awaits.

Be held inside the life-giving waters of resilient compassion.
Let the winds of change become your joy.
Dial into the frequency of self-love that rocks your spirit awake.

Mother self in a soul care way—
holding, listening, embracing tenderness.
Mending, patching, weaving—true nature restored.
Gaia's lifeforce is generative, let her be your guide.
She will teach you how to braid the most delicate and influential
threads into your life's work.

And when fatigued, lay your body upon hers,
and receive the exquisite transmission of renewal.
This grandmother to mother to child healing is part
of the great divine feminine matrix.
We are rising in a new way—can you feel it?
Be ready to answer the call.
Your soul service is ready to be guided
by the pure spirit of the mother.

Practices for
Embodying the Mother

~

Guided Visualization: Spirit of the Earth—
Anchor into Gaia, Enhance Your Frequency

Come as you are, begin where you are. Right here, right now. Take a deep breath in, and a deep breath out. Allow yourself to begin again in this moment. There is nothing to fix, no problems to solve, no goals to reach, nothing from the past or future is preoccupying your mind.

And for this guided journey, give your body permission to soften, breathe deeply now as if you are forming your relationship with the earth right here, right now.

Whether you are lying down or sitting up, begin to feel the pulse of breath inside yourself, and visualize connecting your breath pulse with that of the earth's. Then imagine connecting the rhythm of your heartbeat with the pulse of the wondrous and unlimited source of energy that dwells inside the earth's dark, rich, fertile soil.

Completely relax, step out of this current time frame, and imagine your inner body like a light source magnifying towards your outer body. Begin with your lower body, and visualize a swirling, grounding, anchored root system streaming from your body into the earth. Bring your awareness to your spinal column and allow it morph into the trunk of a tree, or the stem of a flower. Your pelvis is now nourished through the complex yet organized root system into the earth. You are whole and connected. Breathe fully. Soften. Come to your lungs, heart, shoulders and fill this area with the tree's branches, the unfurling of the flower's petals. See the colors, the shapes, the energetic qualities, and merge your consciousness with this life force. Be touched by what you see and feel. Feel the palms of your hands radiate with this life-giving force. Hold the earth, support her alchemy, and feel her strength stream from the palms of your hands in all directions around you.

There is healing in your hands. Breathe fully. Soften once again. Visualize your neck and throat opening to embody the grandeur of the mountains traversing, shape-shifting, clearing, fortifying, merging anew. A call to the ancients, a call to the Gaia life force surrounding you, encouraging you to express all truths now. In the name of this antiquated Mother well: allow words, worlds, symbols, songs, chants, sounds, cries, tears—allow them to freely channel through you. Hold nothing back. There is healing happening now.

Soften. Feel your roots anchoring you into the womb of the earth once again. Relax your forehead, visualize an opening here, you may see a color, a symbol, you may feel an energy, hear a sound. There is nothing to find or seek here. Simply let go and attune to this area for a soft opening or sensation. Now go into the center of your mind, soften, breathe, and feel into your shape-shifting visual capacity. Allow Mother Earth's council to transform limiting mind loops, follow her birth to death to rebirth cycle. What needs to die out of your mind currently? Go deep into another time frame. Go back to your childhood, allow the earth's strength to pull and untangle these limiting experiences, narratives, and patterns out of you now. They are not for you anymore; they are no longer yours. Witness them coming out of you, and morphing, churning, burning, and transforming into the earth's soil, like compost with the force of the sun, the soil is regenerated.

Spaciousness surrounds you. Soften. Breathe.

Open a conversation and ask her how she is today. "Mother Earth, as I touch down, and anchor into you, I honor your abundant capacity to hold and house unlimited life-giving energy. How can I support the earth's vitality today?"

Perhaps a wish, a prayer, a holding of awe and reverence for her striking beauty.

Merge your own source of life-giving energy with the earth's. If you are ready to receive support and counsel from the earth, soften completely, take a deep breath in and out, and allow your body to be a conduit for earth energy. Formulate a conversation: "Spirit of the earth, I am ready and open to receive insight and grounding at this time. As I open myself to soften and anchor, I am awake to the signs, omens, divine timings, and the messengers that cross my path so I may receive the teaching.

"I am enough. I am full. I am whole. I am connected to the earth as a conduit for abundance, growth, and vitality. I regenerate daily. Every day I awake inside the realm of possibility. I am here. I honor my grounded, rooted, and connected self."

As you rise with an inner knowing that you are supported by the earth's greatness, by her abundance, move through your day open and ready to receive the grounding, fortifying, and softening process that lives inside each moment. Your limiting thought process becomes a reminder to breathe deeply and inhabit your body temple once again as an ancient old growth cedar tapping into the earth's expansive wisdom.

And when your body speaks of pain and suffering, listen to hear, soften to see, and return again to your breath in synchronicity with that of Mother Earth and all sentient beings.

Gaia's Daily Activation
Grounding over Fear
Creativity over Overwhelm
Authenticity over Shame
Boundaries over Guilt
Seeing Beauty over Seeing Lack
Compassion over Judgement
Love over Fear
Unity over Separation
Grace over Complexity
Stillness over Immediacy
Being over Doing
Feeling over Thinking
Sensing over Forcing
Receiving over Giving

Create to Heal Your Feminine Frequency

Intention

To clear the ancestral line, enhance your personal frequency and weave a cloak of ancestral honor. To include resistance, repulsion, disconnection, illusion, and delusion. To acknowledge that pain and love untangle the toxic hooks of ancestral shame. To raise your compassionate frequency.

Set your intention: choose your space and medium, gather supplies and plan a time frame to activate this creative healing ritual.

Move your body or sit in meditation to clear your mind.

Light a candle to create sacred space.

Paint, draw, collage, vision board, speak, dance, or journal the aspects within you and your ancestry that you wish to release and heal.

Do the same for the aspects you choose to honor and carry forward.

Reflect on what came through and name three calls to action to support this newfound frequency.

Gaia's Source: Walking Meditation

Intention

To deepen your connection to the earth and welcome the feelings of abundance, connection, and deep nourishment.

Find a peaceful place in nature where you can walk in silence, barefoot if possible.

Turn off your electronic devices.

Set an intention to release feelings of lack, unworthiness, fatigue, disconnection, and stress.

Soften your whole body and release all expectations, along with all roles and responsibilities.

Each step you take, imagine pouring love from the soles of your feet into the earth, while simultaneously receiving the love back from the earth.

Allow any thoughts to be released without forming any judgements about them.

Let your hands become generators of energy—pour love from your heart into your hands and from there into the earth and all her creations. Receive this abundance back into your hands and swirl it through your whole body.

Imagine or sense a color, vibration, or pattern aligned with the earth's essence and invite it to merge into your body. Let this feeling ground into the earth and flow through your body out into the world.

Observe how you feel and integrate this into your life.

A Mother's Gifts

The Mother is intuitively aware of the seasons, rhythms, and messengers that live inside nature's divine creations. Her body matrix, mind temple, and ancient understanding of the cycles of creation allow her to dance with all energies around her. She expands her vision through autumn leaves, winter's darkest night, spring's blossoms, and summer's endless harvest.

The embodied Mother tracks time based on her natural environment. She flows with the bird's migration routes, self-regulates with the lunar cycle, senses a storm brewing, receives the nourishing rains, and attracts the pollinators to her garden.

The earth's vitality is aglow in her eyes, the steadiness in her gait is to be trusted, her calming presence feels like a warm embrace. The embodied Mother works in union with Gaia, protecting and igniting the divine order in all living things. She maneuvers through the portals of life, death, and rebirth like stepping on stones across the river of life.

Embodied to the core, her frequency
of love rises above anything steeped in lack or fear.

The Mother's reciprocal ways of releasing and inviting life
force energy keeps her steady through any storm.

Journal Prompts to Embrace the Mother's Gifts

Characteristics of the Embodied Mother
Compassionate | Resilient | Aware | Steady | Resourceful
Fertile | Abundant | Nurturing

What are you growing tired of? What is dying out of you?

What happens in your body when you get overwhelmed?

Write out the physical sensations when you get overwhelmed and fearful or feel a negative charge in your body.

What practices bring you out of fear or overwhelm and into calm?

In what ways can you commit to loving your body as your sacred temple?

What is birthing alive in you right now?

What life cycle are you currently in: planting, growing, birthing or harvesting?

Journal about this cycle, and how it may naturally grow into the next one to complete your vision.

If your soul had a song, a poem, a prayer for the future, a longing, a desire—what would that be?

Journal Prompts to Reveal the Mother's Shadow

Characteristics of the Mother's Shadow
Co-dependent | Over-giving | Under-receiving
Victim/Martyr Complex | Depleted

Name the wounds you carry from your ancestry.

Describe how it manifests in your current life.

Name the ways, if any, that you disassociate from your body or bypass your own needs.

What actions can you take to begin the healing for positive change?

Do you play the victim or the martyr in your life? If so journal about where this shows up in your life, and how you can interrupt the process.

What does your inner child want to say to you right now? Imagine her being safe, filled with love, joy and playful energy. Is there something she is longing for? How can you listen, feel, and greet her with deep compassion? What does that look like and feel like?

Write a decree or an affirmation that will remind you of your sovereignty and capacity to live your life from a place of free agency.

For example:
I am releasing the narrative of addiction, fear, repression of emotions, judgement, criticism and patriarchy from my ancestral identity.

I choose to carry forward my ancestral gifts of compassion, kindness, community, farming, resourcefulness, love, family-first attitude, artistry, and to be a heart-led leader.

Falling

Fall, falling, I'm falling.
Catch me.
The path before, unknown.
The voice within, unfamiliar.

Yet the breath carries on,
a steady pulse of the heart continues,
visions of gratitude feast on nature's cathedral before me.

How is this beauty possible?
Why is darkness so dark?

The rain beats down upon the drunken earth.
The rose bush swirls her silky petals of goodness into the stormy skies.
The golden autumn leaves lose their grip and set themselves free.

No longer holding on.
No longer afraid to fall.
A panoramic view of the ages and stages, cycles, traumas, joys,
births, deaths—alive before me.

And so, I lean in and jump.
I'm falling.

Breathless now, the ice-cold washes over me.
I pray for human to earth to spirit evolution.
I pray for goodness over fear, grace over greed.

There is a revolution stirring here, can you feel it?
In the name of those who have come before,
and those who come next,
do not fear falling or failing or stillness or silence.

And when the dawn stirs,
and shakes you awake breathless and restless—
Sift through the messages in the name of truth and soul's calling.
Fall hard into them, jump holy,
and pray for the human heart to remember what love is.

It will always catch you.
Falling, I'm falling into love.
With you, my heart.
We are falling.

Sage Spirit

"The doors to the world of the wild Self are few but precious. If you have a deep scar, that is a door, if you have an old, old story, that is a door. If you love the sky and the water so much you almost cannot bear it, that is a door. If you yearn for a deeper life, a full life, a sane life, that is a door."

Clarrisa Pinkola Estes

Chapter 3

Sage Spirit
Intuitive Waters Flow

*This living path will always be made of the tender and
the tough. Walk hand in hand with grace and grit. Find
flow inside the murky waters, witness the tides roll in and
out. Gather your treasured lost parts. Be mesmerized by the
incantations of songbirds at dusk. Listen to the pause inside the
pause. Seek many dimensions daily. When faith reaches
a tipping point, welcome your elder wisdom. Take your
Sage's hand and walk her to the acceptance temple.
Look her in the eyes—tell her she is loved, she can rest,
she is safe. Nothing else matters but this moment, now.*

Connecting to Your Inner Sage

Our life's adventures are marked by the crossroads where we
experience change. Releasing of one way of being invites in another
way. As we navigate the highs and the lows, each lived experience
informs the next. Sometimes we react to our life circumstances out
of past conditioning—doing what we think we ought to do. We may
find ourselves repeating patterns that hold us back from living in
alignment with our true nature.

Other times we respond from a place of trusting our gut. We
receive a message, an insight, or an intuitive flash that prompts us to
shift the course of our life. It feels right, fluid and good, like a deep

moment of inner reckoning with self. The Sage flows with change, while staying present to her evolving intuitive process. She cultivates a peaceful inner life while sharing her visionary's wisdom with the world. The sage does not sleep her life into being. Like the healing hands of a grandmother, she gathers her current materials and weaves them into her cloak of knowledge.

This takes conscious work. We can get easily sidetracked by the demands and dramas of daily life. Being a human in this complex world can be exhausting and confusing. At times we can feel completely alone. When our emotional habits rule our daily existence, it may feel like we are swimming upstream. There may be toxic residue from childhood trauma, addiction, lack of clarity regarding life purpose, disconnection from the body, anxiety, and depression. These can inhibit our intuitive capacity and cause low self-esteem or lack of purpose.

To connect with the inner Sage requires a deep listening within, along with conscious, present-moment awareness. We must be willing to understand how the inner critic may be ruling our lives. This is the voice within that overdramatizes life events, or gets caught in over-doing, over-judging, and under-acknowledging personal efforts.

The Sage's shadow keeps her living in the lower frequency of lack, unworthiness, hopelessness, and abandonment. She fears what others think and remains disconnected from her truth. She is unable to be vulnerable out of fear of showing her weakness.

The connected Sage no longer fears change. She does not get swept away in life's dramas, or take things personally. Rather, she is connected to the vast, mature, and refined inner wisdom. The embodied Sage is the observer of energy, the seer of evolution. She is non-judgemental yet precisely discerning. She hungers not for power over others, but for a softer, more potent wisdom. She lives in the balance between listening and speaking, between courageous acts and meditative moments, between comfort in relationship and joy in her aloneness. The sage understands where to place her awareness and when to not get involved in drama.

Meditation

Take a moment to take three full, deep breaths. Soften your jaw, shoulders, and consciously release tension in your body. Visualize that you are standing before a perfectly still lake. Instead of seeing your reflection, you see your elder self—intuitive, connected, ready to support you. This is your inner Sage. Imagine what she looks like, a wise elder version of you. Gaze into her warm eyes, feel her warm smile, hold her beautifully weathered and wise hands.

Your elder Sage spirit is here to guide and support you in every aspect of your life. She will ground you when you go into overwhelm, clear you of emotional debris, and love you just as you are. The Sage's intuitive whispers are the catalyst for clarity and change in all areas of life. No longer fear being lost, unsupported, or alone. Build your relationship with your inner Sage. As you wake each morning, light a candle in her honor, and open your body as a channel to receive this intuitive, peaceful, and wise frequency.

Your inner Sage is here to remind you of your own timeless intelligence. She will empower your natural aging journey, by helping you to observe, discern, and transform the parts that believe you cannot fulfill your greatest visions.

There is nothing to hide or fix— greet your laugh lines with grace, honor your changing body. Each lived experience contributes to your living tapestry. The Sage's elemental power is water: she is the matriarch of softening, surrendering, releasing, and cleansing. The Sage is the healer within. Her ability to work with her emotional process allows her to dig deeper into her soul's calling. The Sage understands that relationships, career, and inner work are all ways to gather and sculpt her embodied true nature—whole, fluid, and comfortable in her skin.

Attune to Your Current Frequency

When we can embody a daily practice of living inside the present moment, we are reminded that each day we have an opportunity to begin again. The art of seeing one's life as a blessing rather than a to-do list can completely alter that course of one's life. When we can shift our perspective away from the mundane and fatigue of the daily grind, we can consciously welcome in the attitude that we awake with a new body and mind each day, and that we can end our day by releasing what no longer serves us. Yes, there will always be hardships, challenges, and grief—yet when we can stay inside the realm of each moment, we are gifted the energy of light and steadiness. We can follow an earthcentric rhythm, equally drawing in or contracting to rest—equally—receiving or extending out or expanding our gifts and gestures to the world. This inner to outer rhythm becomes the formula in attuning to your present-moment frequency.

Imagine your body as a channel of energy. Visualize your thoughts, feelings, desires. See how you perceive, receive, and make meaning out of daily encounters with self and others. The experience of this living, interactive ecosystem inside you is your current frequency. Often complex, sensitive, and delicate, your personal ecosystem requires steady attention, as well as permission to evolve and re-organize when needed. Who you were yesterday is different from who you are today and who you will be in the future.

"Wanna fly, you got to give up the shit that weighs you down."
Toni Morrison

The work of the Sage is to become the witness to your personal frequency. Dial into this frequency each morning as you wake. Weave seeds of attentive compassion and kindness into your body as you journey through your day. Invite in rest and nurturance as you welcome the dreamtime.

Get to know intimately how your inner body feels when your energy is clear, loving, and spacious. Pay attention to the energies of judgement, lack, or fear. You get to tap into your own inner genius. Aligning with your current frequency allows you to receive your intuitive gifts. Through daily practices such as meditation, mindful movement and creative pursuits you will receive direct feedback on your own frequency. You will become aware of any personal emotional debris, limiting thought processes, relationships, and physical ailments that need your attention.

The Sage body is the wisdom body. She will speak directly to you if you are ready to listen.

Once you have a connection to your own frequency, you can begin to direct your awareness and actions towards healing, feeding, and evolving the frequency that matches your true nature. Imagine a color, a landscape, symbol, and something from the natural world that holds a vibration that is magnetic to you. For example, an heirloom rose at the peak of its fullness—exquisitely fragrant and wildly supple, petals like silk. You can welcome this energy or vibration into your own frequency simply by using the power of your imagination. You can close your eyes and visualize this energy swirling into your own body and mind. Where in your body will this frequency support you? How does it land inside you? Is there a message it wants to bring you? Soften to receive it, trust that you will be guided. Let it land and take root inside your body. This alchemical process becomes the living ceremony of enlivening your own frequency while attuning to your intuitive voice.

Trusting Your Intuitive Voice

You may remember a time when you ignored your gut instincts, times when you viscerally felt called to take one path and chose a different direction. You have most likely also experienced those times when you knew that you had to make a difficult life decision—though it involved challenge or hardship for yourself or others—yet you listened because the pull was so potent that you could not choose another way. Learning to listen, feel, and trust your intuition is a lifelong study.

When life gets challenging, which it does and it will, you may find it difficult to feel or hear your psychic ability or sixth sense. Everything else becomes more important—deadlines are real, life's stressors become all consuming—and the tendency to check out due to fatigue and overwhelm becomes habitual. Sound familiar? In order to learn from the past, it can be helpful to reflect on specific times where you ignored your intuitive power.

Scan back through your life and think about the times when you listened to your gut instinct and acted on it. Recognize the sensation you felt in your body, your mind, and in the environment around you. As you begin to remember and study these intuitive recalls, you will form a relationship with your own psychic energy. You will get to understand the body–mind sensations involved and you will be able to discern with more clarity how to trust your instincts.

The deeper work is to sift through your habitual patterns, judgements, and inner critic to understand when they are ruling your life. Discerning the difference between anxiety and intuition is profound and liberating. Anxiety comes with a back story, often infused with past narratives, fears, and stressors. Your intuitive voice empowers what is true in the moment, and does not dwell in comparison of past or current events. Coming back to this one simple question—"what is true in this moment?"—allows you to listen, feel, and live inside your own shape-shifting self.

Compassionately understanding and staying present with your emotional debris allows you to receive insights on how to live a life with clarity and intention. Often, it's about softening and slowing down in order to see what is ready to come through. That's why a meditation or mindful movement practice is wildly supportive in developing your intuitive gifts.

Where do you personally create space for your intuitive energy to awaken? For some, it's found in nature—feeling the winds of change at your back, the purification of your whole body submerged in the ocean, waking as the sun rises, or long quiet drives on country roads. For others it could be that your intuitive voice comes while cooking a meal, painting, meditating, dancing, singing. The creative life is a powerful force allowing the intuitive body to integrate and speak.

When you can maintain a steady connection in body, mind, and heart, naturally you will experience less clutter or dramatic reactionary patterns. Therefore you allow your body to become a channel for truth and insight. Your gut instincts will be able to speak to you more clearly when your gut health is in balance. Your mental clarity increases when you get proper rest and practice mindfulness. Compassion increases when body and mind feel good. There is a positive frequency that expands when you choose curiosity over judgement. When you can rise out of the defensive, overly critical, and victim mentality, you can tap into your personal intuitive process and receive support in life's most challenging moments. This is the work of the Sage—calm, connected and deeply wise like a vast mother ocean generating harmony for all living organisms.

Practice presence over a constant forced agenda. Attune to the moments when a flash of lightning strikes in the form of an idea, luminous clarity, or a surge of faith and devotion. When these unexpected moments arrive, drop everything else and dive into this frequency. This is your intuition speaking directly to you. Notice what you sense, hear, smell, and taste.

Intuitive Listening: A Lifelong Pursuit

Your inner Sage holds a frequency that is higher than the inner critic and steadier than the frantic multi-tasking martyr. Find a rhythm in your day where you connect to your gut instincts. First thing in the morning can be a powerful time for this. It can take just three minutes. Ask your intuition to support your current process, attune to this positive vibration within, and listen to what wants to come through. Often this is not a literal process. You may receive colors, symbols, signs, or images. Receive these signs with curiosity, don't try and make exact meaning out of them. Trust the instinctual frequencies that support your current life process.

For example, as you call for support regarding a particular life situation, you may see a surge of color like a sunset. Or you may see a shape like a spiral coming into a certain place in your body. Sometimes, the image of an animal, bird, ocean or forest comes like a flash to guide you. When these positive frequencies arrive, listen, trust, and invite them in. You don't have to make meaning of anything right away, though you may receive an inspired "aha" that helps you deepen into the work you are meant to be doing at this time.

Journaling your intuitive flashes will support this relationship, as will naming them inside your mind or out loud to yourself or others in a calm and peaceful state. A powerful practice is to ask your inner sage questions in a calm, meditative state before you go to bed.

For example: *Show me the way, am I aligned? Let me feel what is essential for my life's path at this time. What is the highest goodness here? Is this what I truly want?*

Allow the questions to simply be, without looking for answers. Adopt an attitude of vast openness, nonjudgmental awareness, and quiet expectancy.

As you wake in the morning, you may receive insights from your dreams or from the questions you asked yourself the night before. Write them down as soon as they arrive. Without imposing your will or judgement, simply welcome any insights, messages, or shifting frequencies. Observe how your body feels. Specifically get connected to your lower abdominal and low back area. The more you can feel connected to this area as a source of health, love, and power, the more you will be able to clearly receive an intuitive message. No longer will you feel drained emotionally. Your internal dialogue will become more positive, you will become more inspired and efficient in the work you do.

My inner elder nudges me to shed layers. Naked and tender,
I spiral into liminal space. Dancing into the unknown, I am
drawn into the dark waters. I stand in sovereignty of mind
and body and soul. "Anything is possible," she whispers.

Reveal the Sage's Shadow

The active and compassionate Sage is guided by her intuitive, resourceful, and calm nature. However, when the Sage is shadowed, she is unable to tap into her insightful, enlightened, and understanding capacities. In her darkness, the Sage is readily confused, fraught by the decision-making process, frightened, and resistant to change. She fears her own success and does not believe in her innate wisdom. The shadowed Sage feeds her inner critic and plays small inside the limiting self-paradigms. Her unresolved emotional patterns from the past continue to rule her daily existence. Due to patriarchal and ancestral trauma, she resists the healing of her inner masculine, which leaves her feeling depleted. She follows others as opposed to leading from a place of free will and a healthy, balanced ego.

We can all relate to living in the Sage's shadow at certain times in our life. When we experience the shadow, we can choose to reject or repress it. Or we can see it for what it is and get curious, asking why it is surfacing and how we can transform it. The aim is to reveal the shadow, track its origin, and compassionately call upon the inner Sage for guidance.

What we often find is emotional debris from the past. The inner critic and the false egoic identity strive to persuade us that we are not good enough, not worthy, and will never be successful. It's inside this paradox of the mind's dual nature that we must discern how to feed the "wisdom self" over the "victim self." When our daily existence is clouded by guilt, shame, and fear, there is no space for the intuitive voice to be heard. That is why the work of tracking emotions is essential in order to allow the Sage to speak.

Naming Emotional Debris: Empowering Vulnerability

Discerning what no longer serves you will ultimately guide you towards the frequency of your own signature essence and true calling.

All too often the pace of our busy lives does not leave room for us to name and understand the influence that emotional debris from the past has on us. The colonial drive to do more, accomplish more and never rest generates an inner atmosphere of stress, imbalance, and often overwhelm.

When the Sage's shadow is ruled by emotional debris and unresolved guilt, your creative capacity and your intuitive process shut down. The body and mind become a vessel of fight or flight or freeze tendencies. The inner critic gets louder than anything else and we lose our ability to navigate life with a clear and calm vibration. This may be a coping mechanism learned as a child or inherited from traumatic experiences in our family's past. It's important to understand your own Sage's shadow and to name why it exists. If, for example, as a child you were taught that good children don't cry and don't speak their opinion, then you abandoned your own vulnerability at a young age. Now is the time to gather all your lost parts and pieces.

Simply naming our deeper emotional states allows us to recognize why we feel the way we feel. This requires vulnerability and self-acceptance. When we feel trapped in a particular emotional field—when guilt, shame, fear, or grief gets a grip on us—our habitual pattern may be to ignore, repress, or dull its impact. Yet when we can pause to feel and name the emotional debris, we can more fully understand what triggers us into this state. When we engage in the frequency currently running though the body and mind, we see how to become vulnerable enough to meet the shadow within. So instead of repeating statements like "I am so overwhelmed, I will never get my work done" or "I can't trust my instincts because I am afraid I will be wrong" we can acknowledge that this is a habitual pattern. We understand how it is not a supporting frequency. In fact, it's a debilitating vibration that will continue to rule both your mind and your actions in the world.

The root of vulnerability is our willingness to show our true emotions to be seen and our weakness to be known. The virtues of honesty and trust are the cornerstones of open and meaningful conversation.

Whether this conversation is with your inner self or with your loved ones and colleagues doesn't matter; the mature Sage understands the art of naming states without overdramatization in order to clear the energetic field. Once the field is clear, the Sage can let go of attachment to any imbalance or forced outcome and move on with more efficiency and ease.

The call of the Sage is to take time for self-care, to reset your nervous system often, to honor flow over force, and to create space for reflection over constant productivity. Creativity grows when we step inside a lifestyle balanced between rest to activation. Dwelling on what is good and positive in life generates an aligned attention to what is working as opposed to what isn't working. When we can turn inwards and meet the eyes of the wise elder with vulnerability, we can transform our emotional debris into compassionate understanding. Herein lies the mastery of the activated Sage—vulnerable, intuitive, and discerning.

The Power of Choice: A Sage's Tool

How we process, manage, and work with the power of choice is the foundation of our experience. Every decision we make reflects the overall outcome of our life. The human journey is about discerning what we want to create and what we need to survive, how to fulfill our desires and express our innate gifts. Learning how to discern the current energies we are faced with will support our decision-making process. However, if there is unresolved guilt or excess emotional debris, fear of making the wrong decision clouds the process. "Yes," "no," or "I don't know yet" all become muddled into "what if?," "what should I do?," or "maybe I should do that instead?." We can become emotionally and mentally paralyzed.

If the power of choice is taken away from us at an early age, for example, if our parents made all our decisions or we were not allowed to speak our own truth and fulfill our healthy desires, our decision process was not properly exercised. In response we may have created a pattern of not trusting our own instincts and seeking others to make choices for us. Naming our past and present narrative around how we come to make decisions will empower our choices based on who we are today.

Honoring choice as an energetic frequency, while welcoming the state of flow, will, over time, activate our intuitive pathways. Once the awareness around personal choice awakens, we can train our brains to re-route the distorted chatter of the inner critic and connect with what we really want and what matters most. Getting curious about what motivates our choices and tracking this process is a powerful tool. For example, in a decision-making process, we can ask ourselves, "Am I making this choice based on fear or faith? Love or control? Authenticity over martyrdom? Truth or illusion?"

We can further this process by getting in touch with the center of our bodies. Here lies the *intuitive messenger*. Our lower abdominal area, low back, and womb space are places where the emotions of guilt and shame often get stored. Also, the place where we spent nine months in our mother's womb, the center of our bodies, can become a place of paradox. Here we have grown our children or our creative projects and experience our monthly cycles. Society tells us as women to suck it up and in; being slim in the waist and curvy in the hips is desirable. Instead of adorning the abdominal life-giving area, we receive the message to change, fix, or hide it. Yet our gut instincts are the messenger of both fear and flow, and where our intuition is sparked. This is why it's essential to feel, hear, and sense what our gut wants to tell us. Retraining the brain to honor the power we hold and create in our center body is the key to lasting self-acceptance. It's a deeply life-altering experience when we can connect to our essential self in this way. The Sage wisdom lives in our centers.

Imagine the whole body as an ecosystem. When there are afflictions in the body and mixed messaging in the mind, then the ecosystem must fight to survive. Some pockets of energy hold more stress, fear, and anxiety than is necessary. This energetic state then rules the mind and blocks the fluid state of balance; our instincts become abandoned, questioned, or not even considered. Getting clear on personal morals and ethics will also support the flow inside the body. Mindful practices and conscious living enhance our capacity to discern what we want and what we don't want. This changes throughout our life. When we can stay present to our shape-shifting bodies and minds, personal boundaries become clearer. We can readily attune to our highest self and share it with the world.

Learning what motivates our choices is a potent inquiry for the Sage's evolution. Understanding that there is both positive and negative reasoning, we see that our choices originate out of the duality of opposites. Again, there is a paradox here: the duality of choice and control. When we over-control every aspect of our lives, we may struggle with disappointment or an imbalanced expectation of self or others. This then leads to the fear of letting go and living inside the natural state of flow. When we loosen our grip of perfection and success, what does that feel like within? Why do we need to hold on so tightly? Is it because we fear change, or are we attached to always having to look and feel a certain way?

When we can understand and trust that change is in fact the rhythm of life, we can more readily welcome change. Fluid as a winding river, ephemeral like cloud formations, the earth's epic beauty reminds us of our capacity to evolve. The shape-shifting fire warms the Sage's hands. This elemental perspective assists us in letting go while welcoming a positive frequency inside the present moment. Sourcing inspiration from the natural world reminds us how to build steady and authentic inner strength.

Through this lens, we discern what is delusional, controlling, and materialistic or based only on external power. When we begin any decision-making process by turning within, before we seek external validation, the Sage becomes more embodied. This leads to greater awareness of how essential it is to work with our current emotional, relational, and mental states. Thus we become moral humans, living harmoniously and humbly inside the power of choice, not only for ourselves, but as part of a collective consciousness to better the world we live in.

What am I unwilling to see?
What do I truly feel?
I needed to get lost, in order to be found.
And when I opened my eyes, everything had shifted.
A birthing alive is an electric process.
Newfound softness, a surrendered gaze, an empowered inner Sage.
Memories burst forth like poplar buds in the spring.
An unforgettable resonance of sweetness pulls me closer.
Lean in, my elder whispered,
and to the wild river I return.
To feel her fully, holy, is to feel her
reborn once again—inside me.

A Sage's Process:
Pillars of Creativity to Activate Intuitive States

One intentional way to activate intuitive states is through the creative process. This is a wildly rich, deeply curious, and endless discovery.

There is always a healing that takes place when you engage in creative pursuits. The light peers through the crack into another time and space, your intuitive powers ignite, and you go forth with a renewed perspective. Your vision is inspired by the goodness that surrounds you.

The "Pillars of Creativity to Activate Intuitive States" is a five-step method to engage in any life pursuit, creative endeavor, major life decision, or desired activation. Use it as a formula to organize chaos into form, confusion into clarity, and overwhelm into intentionality.

I. Intention

Begin by getting clear on your intention. Ask yourself: What is the essence of what I want to create, manifest, embody, or activate? Consider in your vision how your offering will benefit the greater good of humanity. What will this give back to the world? The shorter your intention the better. One succinct sentence as an affirmation is most powerful. Write this down, share it with a trusted friend or colleague.

2. Presence

Remind yourself that present-moment awareness inside your creative process is gold. Weave your intuitive voice into your project. Bring forward the ways in which you will leave space for your gut instincts. Reflect on how this intuitive voice may differ from the practical, rational, critical, and literal voice within. Create space for all the voices and sentiments to come through, then discern where the overly dramatic, reactionary and fear-based thinking and feeling takes over. Journal about this, name it, so you can see where your egoic, tricky mind wants to keep you playing small. Your present-moment awareness allows you to see more clearly what your drama self is and what is your intuitive power.

3. Compassion

Form a relationship with the virtue of compassion. Let this energy of kindness, forgiveness, and non-judgement be at the core of your creative pursuit. This will allow for a more expansive perspective on the project. You will evolve your intuitive frequency when you can disrupt the inner-critic patterns. Catch yourself when you are repeating phrases such as: "I am always . . . I am never . . . I won't be able . . ." Be a kind observer of these lower frequencies. Without judgement, detach yourself from them, understand this is your ego trying to control the outcome, return to your breath, and then see what is currently working inside your process. This shift in seeing the positive will reset your nervous system, while connecting you more compassionately to the current process. Intuition flows more freely when you are not in constant reactivity. Welcome in peaceful, clear energy and trust that this will get you closer to your overall vision.

4. Action

Throughout the time of your creative process, whether it be short or long, you may receive a call to be in direct service to your intention. This can come through like a lightning bolt or it may feel like connecting to the deeper roots of what will serve your purpose in life. Open yourself to receiving these moments, often fleeting, like glimmers, or the quickened pace of a shooting star. If we are not awake inside our process, they will be missed. Stay open to change inside the call to action. The creative process is like finding the stones to cross the river. When you finally get to the other side, your original intent or vision may have been altered by your journey. When you can release your stubborn, egoic need to complete things, your creative pursuits can become fully realized. Surrender or soften to the outcome and allow the unknown, mysterious and surprising calls to action to come forward. Again, the key is trusting in the process.

5. Accountability

To commit to your creative vision, you must persevere in a way that is productive. Staying accountable to your process by sharing with a friend, scheduling specific times in your calendar, or tracking your journey by journaling will magnify your personal frequency. As you recall and refine your core intentions along with a vision that anchors you towards giving back to the collective, you will live in a reciprocal relationship with the world. Stay present to your desire to be over-productive or to the inertia that leads to procrastination. It's a fine balance to strike, sometimes you over-do, other times you under-do. The work is to anchor into right action, while aligning with both the intuitive and the present-moment practical reality. At times it feels like riding a sweet wave, other times like swimming upstream. Cultivating a relationship with your intuition inside any creative pursuit or life project will always serve the greater goodness inside the vision. Then you can witness the gifts of your process evolve into what they are meant to become.

Practice the art of observing your life through the lens of timelessness. Patience is a virtue. The powers of divine timing and right action support you. Be nourished by the elemental womb of land to sea, sky to sun; these exquisite creations teach us how to live intuitively. Drink in the elemental beauty, embrace the softness and vulnerability replicated in nature's divine design. Allow the moon's luminosity to lead you when you are lost.

This is pure source sharing ancient stories in present time. Be guided by rivers, oceans, streams, and lakes, bridge your consciousness towards a gracious surrender to the fluid design of all living things. Like Isis, be the bestower of visionary leadership, the carrier of intuitive light.

The holy waters will hold you in grace; they will release you when you are ready for the next adventure. Look up, expand your mythic wings, the infinite sky's shape-shifting ways will purify your vision time and again.

Mythic Connection:
Goddess Isis, a Visionary Legend

The Egyptian goddess Isis has been revered as one of the most empowered and influential goddess figures in history. Known as the goddess of fertility, and associated with rebirth and the moon's mysterious enigma, Isis is guided by her intuitive insights and her inner visionary powers. Her Sage-like ways were known to weave the virtues of oracular insight, faithfulness, inner beauty, and spirituality. Isis is often seen with the wings of a hawk soaring her into new depths and dimensions. She follows the moon for spiritual guidance and holds bloodstone and amethyst to anchor her into both the sacred and the mundane of everyday life. In her wise and accessible ways, she was known to the people of Egypt as the goddess of rebirth, medicine, and magic. Isis was personified as the seer of all, the one who was in complete flow with all she crossed paths with. She was known to be able to support and protect others as they journeyed into the realm of the dark underworld.

In our modern life, we can call upon the goddess Isis to channel our intuitive capacities and to help us remember that we are wise leaders of both the practical daily world and the spiritual, magical world. We can recognize and reflect the depth of our relationships as medicine of love to share across the cosmos. To dream our life into being is the realm of Isis's power. When your energy feels depleted, and the Sage within retreats to her inner critic, call upon Isis to remind you of your own capacity to create, generate, and bring to completion projects with an intuitive steadiness. Feel her hawk wings anchor into your heart. Call to Isis before you sleep and ask for your dreams to bring you closer to your soul purpose. Honor the monthly lunar cycle for inspiration, lay down the lower frequencies of doubt, fear, and guilt. Remember that you too can be a visionary leader, meeting your communities with the heart and soul of Isis's magic.

As the wild river within meanders towards unification and interconnectivity, surrender to feel the purification of mind and body. Allow your tears to bless the earth. A cleansing initiation opens the floodgates to receiving the paradoxical pulse of both the cosmic and steady. Your truth awaits you. Welcome the flow inside all the changes. Be ready to embrace the highest, most humble, and wisest version of you.

Befriend Your Elder Wisdom

To feel, heal, and stay authentic, you need to move, write, and create with unapologetic expression. When you give yourself permission to flow inside your current life process, you become a witness to your own emotional range. This allows you to sift through your current state and let go of thoughts, feelings, and desires that no longer serve you. Making choices to allow outmoded frequencies to flood out of you becomes easier when you are grounded and present. You no longer need to be ruled by life's rollercoaster of events. Shape-shifting is your birthright. Your intuitive channels are your superpower. It's time to receive the matrix of fluidity, and to honor water as a source of potent healing.

Greet yourself the way your best friend would; this is your Sage wisdom landing home. Let yourself be kindred to *you*. Lay down your guard. Be the fool in the name of vulnerability. Honesty is a practice; perfectionism is toxic. Surrendering your ego in the name of truth will keep you authentic. Join hands with your inner Sage, she will guide you home on the darkest nights, enchanting you with medicine hymns to soothe your tired heart and ease your fragmented mind.

You will feel your inner Sage come alive. She is the one who stops you in your tracks, flashing her torch to awaken you. Re-route and receive the messages coming through. She feels like a cinematic flash, a sense of another presence, a voice that says *"yes,* go forward," or *"no,* hold back." The Sage will free you of backstories and past conditions. Drama is not her medium. Timeless, universal wisdom is her North Star. With precision and patience, she untangles herself from guilty residue and the voice of the inner critic. Her sacred cloak heals old wounds into awakened dreams and a remembered destiny. The Sage is the bearer of divine timing—a calling, a whisper, lighting flash, thunderbolt crash, volcanic rumbles, atmospheric rivers, a distant roar of change. The Sage listens and discerns truth inside the presence of each moment. Just as our own life seeds are generated inside our great-grandmother's womb, this unique legacy in you is longing to be expressed.

Befriend your elder capacity, trust your gut, no longer fear aging. Process your pain until it begins to dissolve back into the mouth of the mother ocean. The Sage's intuitive powers hold a frequency of potent healing alchemy. Acknowledging this elder presence within is like transforming a single tree into an abundant forest. It not only supports your evolution, but it also benefits the greater good of humanity.

Practices for Embodying the Sage

Receive Your Sage Wisdom: Guided Visualization

Connect to your breath and welcome an energy of light into your whole body—as if the sun is beaming down upon you. Allow your whole body to soften into receptivity.

Begin to release your daily concerns, to-do lists, challenges and preoccupations. One by one, name them and give them over to one of the elements: water, earth, air, or fire.

As you untangle your mind from thoughts of lack, criticism, and judgement, observe how you feel. Go deeper. Sense the frequency of your current self. Allow your whole body to relax, and welcome spacious and peaceful breathing.

Now, visualize your elder self sitting before you. If this is challenging, choose an elder who could be a supportive guide or ancestor. Open to receiving counsel from this elder's wisdom. Look her in the eyes. See the Sage's timeless knowledge and beauty emanating through her whole body.

You may have questions to ask your elder. "Am I on the right path? What would support me at this crossroads in my life?" Allow any information exchanged to flow through each of you. This is your inner Sage speaking directly to you. Unconditionally, she is supporting you on every step of your journey. She has always been here for you, and now it's time to rekindle your connection.

Now ask your elder to take you on a healing journey. Allow any images or sensations to arise. Stay open to the first impulse of healing and activation within the elements—water cleansing, earth grounding, fire transformation, air purification, or ether spiritual recalibration. On this journey you may receive symbols or signs. There may be other guides, animals, or landscapes to support you on your healing journey. Your Sage wisdom may want to channel the releasing through words, songs, or sounds. You may experience old thought patterns being cleared or painful emotions being released.

As you complete your journey, you may receive a gift or an affirmation to seal in the medicine and the healing.

When your journey is complete, come back into your body, attune to your breath. Visualize once again your elder sitting before you. See the warm glow and soft love in her eyes. Your inner Sage is here to remind you that you are safe, that you can rest, and that you have all the answers you need. You are the medicine woman, the wondrous child, and the intuitive elder. Embody this healing frequency—your essence is vast, wise, and calm.

Journal about your experience. Share it with a friend. And welcome this energetic frequency into every aspect of your life.

A Sage's Blessing

Intention

To restore intuitive capacity, recalibrate personal frequency and empower your true nature.

Place one hand on your heart, and one hand on your lower abdominal area.

Focus on a soft, fluid and nourishing breath. When you feel calm, read this blessing at least three times to yourself.

> *I am the Sage within. I trust that my current process is the teaching I am meant to receive at this time. I honor my body as my timeless temple. I welcome my inner critic as a messenger to clear my mind of lack, confusion, and unworthiness. I let go of all things I cannot control at this time. Vulnerability and attentive listening are my way to walk hand in hand with my*

intuition. Like the holy rivers feeding the mother ocean, I stay fluid inside the great mystery of life. I call upon my guides and the forces within the natural world for support. I am not alone. My hands and heart are warmed by the wisdom carriers that came before me, and those who will come next. I cast my compassionate energy freely across the universe. I am attuning to my soul frequency in this moment. I welcome my inner elder home—trustworthy, wise, and expansive.

Return to this blessing as needed or try writing your own blessing for the healing at this stage of your life, as if your inner elder is writing it for you and to you.

~

Intuitive Sage Activation:
Breathe, Pause, Reflect

Intention

To slow down, connect to the breath and the present moment, and welcome your intuitive nature.

This practice is best done after moving the body, getting exercise, breathing fresh air, and releasing excess energy. This helps clear the mind.

Find a place where you can relax and rest your body. Connect to a quiet and comfortable space within.

Set an intention to welcome in your inner Sage—your intuitive wisdom.

With each inhale: Invite in calm and your inner listening powers. Welcome in the power of your intuition.

With each exhale: Release past or future thoughts, let go of the daily stressors, and return to a deep breath.

As you let go, completely soften all the muscles in your body, and pay attention to the pause between each breath. Become calm as you witness, feel, and connect to the pause.

Invite your intuition to join you now inside the pause, as the breath continues to flow, and reflect now on what your Sage wisdom may be wanting to share with you.

It may be a message, a feeling or sensation, or an image. If nothing arises, trust that your connection to your intuition is now activated.

Journal about your experience.

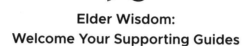

Elder Wisdom:
Welcome Your Supporting Guides

Intention

To welcome support systems through the physical and sacred channels.

Light a candle.

Sit in silent reflection, connect to your breath, and let go of past or future thoughts or desires.

Visualize yourself being completely supported in your life. An element, a symbol, the face of a teacher or elder may come to you. Welcome the guides, teachers or signs that allow you to feel safe and supported to do the work that is essential now. Without forcing, projecting, or attempting to make sense of anything, simply allow the support to be felt on the inside of your body. Like light beams, let it come into you, and see what body parts it lands in. There is a potent healing opportunity when we can track where the body needs the energy. Stay at that place, visualize light, or another color or symbol penetrating this area as you breathe fully and deeply. All other parts of you can soften and let go.

Now welcome your guides as if you are all sitting in a circle together. There may be an exchange of gifts or words. Receive wholeheartedly the supportive messages coming through.

Journal about your experience.

~

Wounds as Wisdom:
A Water Ritual for Inner Transformation

Intention
To honor your wounds and release them to the water for transformation. This can be done alone or in a group setting.

Location
Bath, shower, lake, stream, ocean, or any water source available.

Preparation
Gather items from nature like seasonal flowers, or sacred items like crystals or oracle cards. Create an altar dedicated to healing. Light a candle. Take a few calming breaths.

Call forth your wounds—the heartaches, past traumas, the inner critic, the toxic habitual patterns—as transformational material towards evolving the wisdom within. Name their origin. And trust that the time has come to release them.

Now elicit the ways in which you can free yourself from these old wounds and their control over you. Compose one or more positive affirmations that express the wisdom of your liberation. Journal these sentiments or speak them aloud.

Bring your altar or offerings beside the water for cleansing and renewal. Repeat your affirmations as you immerse your whole body and head into the water. Stay in the water for as long as you can—releasing the old and welcoming your innate wisdom. Soften into every cell of your body. Trust in the empowerment of your natural Sage.

Seal your ritual by giving thanks to the water, earth, fire, and air that holds you in your wisdom and keeps you awake inside the presence of your own healing process.

Share your insights and make a commitment to three nourishing acts you can do in the coming week to enliven this new energy.

~

Body–Mind Mapping:
A Creative Movement Journey

Intention
To shake off stress, shape-shift toxic residue in the mind and body, and embody new pathways of intuitive wisdom.

Find a track of music that truly inspires you to move and be free.

Be in sacred, undisturbed space for at least 10 minutes.

Have your journal nearby. Bring to your awareness repetitive thought patterns or behaviors that are rooted in a negative frequency. Either write them down or express them aloud so they can be acknowledged and released in your movement journey.

Begin by lying down. For at least one minute let your breath be your primary focus while you allow your body to be completely supported by the earth.

Before you begin to move your body, call forth an intention to release what is ready both in mind and body, and to weave together your inner channels to spark rejuvenation, clarity, and intuitive awareness.

When you feel ready begin to follow any impulse to move. You may want to shake, crawl, moan, howl, roll, writhe, rock, jump, or slither. There may be repetitive movements and sounds that want to come out. Let yourself get wild. Completely release all thought patterns. You may work up a sweat, find yourself in tears, or laugh uncontrollably. Trust your movement journey.

When you feel yourself coming to completion, find one place to be in stillness for at least three minutes. Welcome this mind–body calibration. Observe how you feel and welcome any insights in mind and body.

A two-minute free-write is a powerful way to close your session, highlighting any shifts and calls to action received in your body–mind mapping journey.

Healing the Masculine to Live a Sovereign Life: A Free-Write Discovery

Light a candle, have your journal ready.

Find a calm and quiet space within, welcome your elder self for honest reflection and compassionate healing.

Visualize the span of your entire life and connect to the masculine energy in your life's history. What was your relationship like with your father? Or other masculine relationships?

Open the channels from head to heart. Allow any memories, experiences, and belief systems or behaviors to arise and investigate what may be blocking or limiting your current life.

How can you empower your inner masculine self to make choices based on what is good for you? How can you free yourself from past conditioning to live the life you desire?

Finally, imagine how your inner feminine and inner masculine might unify to accelerate your current life vision and empower the wisdom of your intuitive leadership. What daily practices can inspire and support this unification of consciousness within?

Do a five-minute free-write on your discoveries, and call forward an "I am _____" affirmation to guide your inner Sage into balanced and steady embodiment.

Journal Prompts to Embody the Sage

The Embodied Sage's Characteristics
Intuitive | Observant | Humble, Listening
Non-judgemental | Peaceful | Inquisitive

Is there a feeling, sensation, or rhythm in your body when your intuitive nature speaks to you?

Free-write an experience where you felt your intuition calling, and you acted upon this.

Do you have a Sage mirror (a trusted friend or family member) in your life that you can be completely vulnerable with? Who is it?

Task: Find a trusted friend, family member, or counselor where you can be Sage mirrors to one another. Make an agreement to be non-judgemental and completely open to listening and speaking out of freedom and compassion.

Write a personal affirmation that will support your essential nature and your service to the world at this time.

Practice: Welcome your practical yet radical inner elder. Walk the path of truth, cultivate intuition, and connect to daily practices that rekindle fluidity inside your true nature. Befriending self the way you would your best friend is the Sage's superpower.

Journal Prompts to Reveal the Sage's Shadow

Shadow Characteristics of the Sage
Judgemental | Resentful | Imbalanced
Disoriented | Overly Critical

What emotional debris is currently draining your energy?

Where, if ever, do you ignore your gut instincts?

Where does your inner critic hold you back from pursuing your life's desires?

Write down your top three limiting core beliefs about yourself.

Track each one's origin, get curious about how this belief is currently ruling your life.

Rewrite three positive core beliefs or gratitudes about your current life situation.

How do you feed your "victim self" over trusting your "wisdom self"?

Journal what is not currently working in your life. What practices can support you to change what is not working?

What Is This Liminal Space That Graces the Earth?

Everything is energy, the mystics say.
Space in between all spaces, in-breath, pause, out-breath, pause.
Light, pause, darkness, pause.
Movement, pause, stillness, pause.
In this life-death-rebirth cycle of all things, get to know the
pause in between. This threshold is like a rocket ship
of transportation. A shooting star disappears into the dark
night sky. You will miss it if you are looking down.
Be restless enough until you are still once again.

There, the door swings open, an invitation
to enter another time and space.
It will always be different. The colors shift before you.
Your heart pulses faster. Yet this is a new story.
It feels good and right.
Wait inside the still point until leaves morph into a new shade of
their own dimension. Listen to the cue.

The Sage speaks: "You are ready now, here is the key, step into this
channel of reflective light. You are the seer inside this space."

The mystery will always dwell inside the sophistication of the
stars. You are the stardust. Complex, ancient, fleeting like the
ephemeral invitation inside this liminal space.

It's yours to witness. Call it in every morning as the sun rises,
give thanks every evening as the sun sets.
Dreamtime to real time, be true to the call of your intuitive soul.
You are the seer inside this space.

The Huntress

*"When I dare to be powerful—to use my strength
in the service of my vision, then it becomes less and less important
whether I am afraid."*

Audre Lorde

Chapter 4

The Huntress

Visionary, Activist, Warrior Spirit

Ember's glow inside this warrior spirit.
No longer a lonely Huntress—Kali, Lozen,
Oya, Artemis—at Goddess speed.
Guide me as I track the origin of my soul's radiance.
Alchemize my wounds into gifts.
Re-route, pivot, the scent of right action blazes the trail wide open.
Stepping freely into the playground of my evolving consciousness.
Armor peels away to fortify visionary instincts.
Permission given to self and others to live their wildest existence.
Trusting the spiraled cycle of love and pain as the timeless healer
inside all worldly happenings—this is the Huntress matrix.
In service to this calling, my life's work becomes my daily craft.
A deep bow, and a vow to no longer abandon.
A fierce grace ensouls this Huntress body, an unforgettable strength.
A legacy of peace continues to burn golden
into the hearts of all she holds.

Who Is the Huntress?

The embodied Huntress has the true spirit of a warrior and empowers herself and others to live life to the fullest. Her life purpose is fueled by her devotion to be in service to her impassioned cause. The Huntress teaches us how to ignite our true essence and share it unapologetically with the world. This inner fire, once stoked, is peaceful yet fierce, clear, and adaptable. The Huntress spirit has a wild and vast range, which always remains connected to its source. From embers to a blazing fire, the potent energy within the Huntress continues to evolve. The core of your esteemed nature, what lights you up, what stirs your soul, what truly motivates you to stand in your truth is the inner Huntress.

The Huntress is tethered to her inner strength, not only ruled by her mind. And like a skilled warrior, she intuits when to act with clear precision. A connected peripheral vision combined with attuned gut instincts guides her to move from clear willpower and healthy ego. She is committed to facing her fears head on, and understands how to manage her own energy body. In the face of any challenge, she holds the Zen-like key of in-sourcing rather than out-sourcing, reaching within rather than reacting defensively.

The awakened Huntress honors the path of self-transformation by making medicine out of pain or hardship. The death of old egoic ways and outmoded societal paradigms allows her to stay contemporary in her evolving journey. She is the fire igniter, the one who sustains the passion for her cause. She welcomes others to warm their hands and heal their hearts by her fire. She understands the precise moment where her ego needs to die out of her and begin again. As she tends to her inner temple of self-care, the Huntress never hungers or thirsts—she knows exactly how to fuel her soul.

The Huntress living in her shadow is ruled by shame, tends to not take risks, and avoids conflict at all costs. She fears rocking the boat in both career and relationships and prefers to stay in her comfort zone. The internal battle in mind and body keeps her shadow strong. This culminates in inner rage and distorted, unclear choices that become externalized as anger, low self-worth, fear, worry, and self-proclaimed victimization. If the Huntress continues to be repressed, frustration, depression, or addiction will be the repeating narrative. She may constantly blame external factors for her unfulfilled life. Her greatest fear is being abandoned if she breaks free, takes risks, and finally stands in her truth.

The shadowed aspect of the Huntress can also manifest in being overly independent. She will not ask for support out of fear of showing weakness or vulnerability. Defensive, she drives herself to keep feeding her ego. She refuses to lose any battle and will sacrifice her core values and her own honesty in order to win.

Working consciously with the shadow, the Huntress holds an evolved feminine frequency that goes beyond the traditional view of being a warrior on the battlefield. At her core, she trusts the wisdom learned through each experience beyond winning or losing. She knows precisely where to place her energy, and how to maintain her strength through the emotional, physical, mental, and spiritual realms.

She does not pursue conflict only to prove herself right nor does she abandon the call of feminine ensoulment in fear of not being strong enough. Rather, she gathers the natural resources in her present life situation as tools with which to craft her life.

Through the committed journey of self-realization and a compelling devotion to the path of service, she embodies a clear, precise, and potent energy. Discerning and redirecting toxic imprints of bitterness, judgement, and anger that arise in life's complexities is one of her superpowers. Seeing beyond illusion and distraction sparks her resourceful intelligence and allows her to see the bigger picture within the sacred hunt of life.

The Huntress takes a stand for justice, truth, equality, human and animal rights, and is a protectress of the earth and waters. She can track the source of both light and darkness inside her work and transform it into momentum and motivation to fight the good fight.

The embodied Huntress lives within you, ready to awaken your wildest visions and birth them into existence. Allow the Huntress to speak to you, listen to her truths, trust you can shape-shift her wildfire ways and ignite her embers when needed. This evolved frequency is evocative and exquisitely feminine—she can look fear in the eyes, transform it into courage, and call on her support systems, tools, resources, and spirited core to ignite the life she is destined for.

What lives inside your warrior's sword?
Is it sheer will, resentment, fear, or is it a well of compassion
to fulfill the greater good on this planet?

Take me to the fire's ritual.
I offer these soul wounds in the name of evolution.
Carried now too long, I shape-shift into the next version of me.
I am free. I am vital. I am the Huntress alive.

When the Shadow Rules: Your Huntress Wake-Up Call

There will be times when we experience inertia, powerlessness, and fear of taking risks. We are unable to change the parts of our life that are desperate for our attention. This is the Huntress being overruled by her shadow. Physically it may feel like a collapse in the center of the body—as if the passion for life we once knew is no longer alive. In the mind, it may feel like self-sabotage, the cyclic mental chatter that repeats some of the core wounds, "I am not enough, I am not worthy, I am not lovable, I am not strong enough, I don't deserve this, I must win, I cannot fail..." These narratives play out in every aspect of life. When the Huntress is shadowed or blocked from true inner power, the emotional roller coaster of forced willpower is palpable and chaotic. This keeps her from truly listening to what she wants, needs, feels, and sees. It is not grounded, and it is unpredictable. What once seemed doable and in control is now overwhelming.

Physically we begin to manifest this narrative inside the body. The body is our greatest storyteller. The shadow can show up as heart palpations, night sweats, excess anger or grief, sugar cravings, and inability to focus, to name a few.

Low self-esteem or lack of passion and fulfillment can morph into anxiety, and we may feel like we are losing the battle inside this one, precious life. We fall into victimization, self-pity, and self-sabotaging behaviors to keep playing small.

Conversely, our shadowed inner power may take on the story of the warrior in constant battle—with everything and everyone. Deeply rooted in the patriarchal, colonial model of the highly competitive masculine, the shadowed Huntress avoids softening in fear of showing weakness. She tends to be overly independent and pushes every boundary with her over-amplified ego, resulting in an unfilled inner power. She avoids being wrong at all costs. One of her greatest fears is in fact being shamed in front of others for not doing enough, not being perfect enough. The fear of being weak or abandoned keeps her outer shell so strong that her inner softness and her true strength never get a chance to be expressed.

This shadow aspect of the Huntress often manifests in the tendency to be defensive, and to always be the one who's right. This lack of vulnerability blocks authentic inner connection and fulfillment. The internal self is in conflict. Repressed emotions morph in potentially toxic or damaging ways. This way of living does not serve our higher self yet continues to feed the victim energy. It diminishes inner fire; our most passionate and sovereign self becomes muddled and easily fatigued.

At some pivotal point in her life, the Huntress living out her shadow realizes she can no longer soldier on wearing the masks of protection she once believed to be her true strength. Over time, the tolerance for living with the shadow becomes unbearable. In this precise moment an epiphany occurs, and a soul wound has an opportunity to be healed. Courage to trust in the unknown shows her a new way of being. A tender yet fierce, compassionate spirit sees much more than the external power. Thus, the Huntress directs her past, present, and future self towards an honest, authentic, and deeply rooted inner strength.

"But come here, Fear.
I am alive!
And you are so afraid
of dying."
Joy Harjo

Tracking the Origin of Fear:
Wrestling Dragons to Ignite Sovereignty

The work of the Huntress warrior may first present itself in the way you battle your own internal dialogue. Getting attuned to what goes on in your mind is the first step towards shifting negative core beliefs. As you wrestle with daily life struggles, you may begin to see how you question your life purpose, diminish your self-worth, repress vulnerability, and ignore your gut instincts. This becomes the material with which the Huntress either becomes empowered or disempowered. The sacred lessons in life involve tracking fear and observing how you turn away from your own intuitive intelligence or become blind to truth.

What if every time you were overwrought by fear, frustration, or anger, you allowed yourself some time to process? If only a micro dose of synergistic awareness . . . What if you were able to take a breath, feel into your body? What if you could name your fears and acknowledge their origin?

This requires present-moment awareness. It guides you to trust your instincts and tend to self-love fires daily in order to wake up to the hooks of past conditioning and societal paradigms. This is the path of the soul warrior. This is for those who are willing to do the work. This is not for the faint of heart.

Holding the vision to disrupt and re-route the negative mind-loops becomes the mission. Like a Huntress on her soul-retrieving journey, she works with the original imprints of the pain, shame, guilt, blame or fear that live inside life's greatest challenges and joys. She understands her anger cannot be suppressed or repressed. She finds safe places to channel it, allowing it to move until it morphs into shape-shifting realizations.

The Huntress teaches us how to sense the kind of fear that protects us from predators, danger, and helps us survive. These primal fight or flight instincts arrive fully embodied at birth—when we feel safe, we are calm and we can rest; when we feel upset, we cry, we want our basic needs met for food and comfort. Fear is a primal human instinct and when it's understood and alchemized, it can bring us the strength and clarity needed to pursue our life visions.

Chaos churns into form, confusion refines into clarity, helplessness evolves into empowered leadership. Be it joy or hardship, grace or grief, the way you choose to tune in daily becomes the turning point inside your soul's inner compass. The trail opens before you, endless possibilities expand your vision. The ember's glow awaits your homecoming. Every time you feel lost, fatigued, and doubt your journey, the scent of the ceremonial fires come alive within and direct you home to replenish your Huntress vision. The work is to trust the process and show up for yourself every day.

The Imprint of Fear in Your History

Can you remember the first time you felt fear as a child? The fear of being left, the fear of not belonging, the fear of not having the right answer or doing something wrong? The fear of not being liked or accepted? These inquiries require your attention and your compassion as an adult. And if right now, you are experiencing a memory, a trigger, or an epiphany, you are on the right track. These recalls may be the exact medicine you are ready to face in your life right now.

The memories of fear seep into our psyches from an early age and stay with us, usually in an unconscious way. These become the catalysts for us to do what we do or not do in life. In our early years, we may have learned to abandon our instincts. We may have experienced the feeling of giving up our free will to be a good little person—to abide by the rules. Yet our caregivers did the best they could.

Vulnerability is both the willingness to show emotion and to allow weaknesses to be seen. If the practice of vulnerability was not modeled as a child, or if we did not feel safe to show our true feelings and ask for support, there is a greater chance that being vulnerable as an adult will be challenging. The work of the Huntress is to track the origin of the imbalance, pain, or difficulty within. Sourcing the story behind the life experience or the trauma allows for compassionate inquiry. It gives permission to release our identity with the limiting narratives so that we can go deeper into our own healing process.

Life's highs and lows, coupled with fears of both the known and the unknown, keep us inside a narrative of lack or scarcity. Until these fears are examined and acknowledged, they will continue to rule our existence. They will capture us inside a story of who we think we should be and want to be. We will continue to live out our lives ruled by fear. Over time, this energy transforms into a coping mechanism that becomes our story. We carry on the best we can, attempting to control, suppress, or reject pursuing things that both excite us and scare us.

This kind of safety net and false protection is self-sabotaging; we fear taking risks to play it safe. We live in fear of failure. Essentially, this is what holds us back from truly expressing our true gifts in the world. A fracture occurs in our personal energy—simultaneously igniting a deep soul longing. This is what creates the feeling of lack of purpose.

What if each morning you acknowledged certain fears, avoidances, dismissals from your deeper calling? What if you put it on the table and acknowledged these undercurrents? Only then can you connect with your inner Huntress. The Huntress of love, community, animals, the children, earth, waters, art—these inspired reckonings will serve your greater purpose.

*Begin each morning with five minutes of quiet
to simply feel into the present moment. Become a receptive channel
for your visions and aspirations for the day.
Hold intentional space to name what is true—
this will override fear-based thinking.
The Huntress enables the sacred hunt through her Zen-like vision.
Conscious living each day is the gateway to embody
the deeper callings within your soul.*

Create space in your day to name what is true. Become attuned to how and when you give away your energy to what is not true. Name the fears, doubts, and worries as they arise, no longer give them power. Align with what you are opening yourself to. This is the material and the frequency in which the Huntress directs her vision. Sourcing emotional sustenance and mind–body nourishment as a fluid, synchronistic, living energy becomes your greatest resource. It could be tending to self-care needs, or the way you connect with colleagues and loved ones. It could be the stranger you smiled to, the homeless person you fed, the causes you stood tall for, or the protest you participated in. Your authentic voice and grounded activation contribute to the reciprocal matrix of the conscious warrior on her awakened mission to make the world a better place.

The planet begs you to do your good work. She asks of you to let go of your inner critic and to live and love deeply. No longer play fool to the illusion of veils, guarding, and surface talk. Go deep into the abyss where the sun's radiance swirls concentric circles around your bones. Call to the ancient ones and ask for guidance. Make commitments in their honor, and when you begin to lose your faith, remember that the Huntress way lies deep inside the earth below your feet, and swirls in the starry night sky above you. It arrives with the ceremonial fires that warm our healing hands, and the swift, fierce, and gracious winds that awaken our hearts.

Hunt and Gather:
Consciously Crafting the Life You Desire

The embodied Huntress tracks the events, happenings, and experiences in her life because this is where she can sacredly hunt and gather the existence she desires. Quick on her feet, clear in her mind, she can untangle fear from instincts, discern clear boundaries, and activate momentous direction. Her way of perceiving, receiving, and crafting within her environment is impeccable. Like the jaguar who sees in the darkest of nights, her primal tracking techniques are powerful. She can follow the scent of her life's pure desires as clues to fulfilling her life's mission. Like the mythic owl—spontaneous, stealthy, and precise—she is the seer inside any situation. Her peripheral vision is turned on. The primal pulse of life's dance of contraction to expansion, feminine to masculine, and darkness to light generates stamina. Like the owl and jaguar attuning to their inner and outer environments, the Huntress keeps her receptive channels alive in daily awareness.

What if we, as a modern culture, engaged in this kind of intentional living? Be it food consumption, tending physical needs, or connecting emotionally or spiritually, can we track, honor, and integrate what we consume, process, and embody? Through the practice of harmony and good will, we become more accountable for our impact upon this earth. We can become land defenders, water protectors, human rights activists. We can advocate for justice for those who are oppressed or victimized. Sacred activism and conscious living become a way of life, and the ripple effect is profound.

When we fuel our passion for activism in this embodied way, our senses come alive, our visions become vast, our path of service becomes more impactful. We experience a deep sense of belonging and connection to our communities. As we attune to how we care for ourselves we generate a balanced ecosystem in our inner life. This anchors us in our greater life purpose. We can consciously contribute to the evolving planetary needs and see beyond our own ego's hunt for short term satisfaction.

By practicing conscious choices and living in the present moment, you can align with the awakened Huntress. Guided by goodness, you follow the trail of sacred activism, impassioned to answer the call of service for both personal and collective evolution. What authentically lights you up feeds the fire of your gifts. Your visions lead you to create the life you desire. No work is lost; all experiences from your past, when cleansed and empowered, inform your true purpose. Be a courageous and compassionate witness to your trailblazing journey.

No longer allow your journey in life to be passive or assumed. This is the call to activate your soul gifts, consciously gather your tools, sacredly hunt your resources, and share your life vision actively, unapologetically with the world.

Mythic Muse: Kali, Goddess of Creation, Destruction, and Revolution

Kali is known as the dark mother goddess of creation, revolution, destruction and rebirth in the Hindu tradition. Kali's darkness slays evil and ignites true power in the name of justice, right action, and goodness. She has the power to dissolve everything except that which cannot be destroyed, which is one's own true essence. To live with devotion to the path of self-love and acceptance, you must engage with authentic and clear "Kaliesque" power. Kali's mythology empowers you to dismantle defensive boundaries and release personal egoic agenda.

When you dance with life in this way, your attachment to how you look and how you are perceived on the outside becomes less important. Old structures or outmoded paradigms readily free themselves from your psychic grip when you connect with Kali as your muse. As if you are awakening from a slumber, you gather your inner power before externalizing or seeking validation. This will happen more quickly when you are practicing the Huntress powers of clearing negative energy within, practicing vulnerability, and connecting to spacious awareness.

The Kali key to our own vast inner power is to peel away the layers of self-identity and egoic sludge to get to the naked truth. Herein lies the catalyst for true creativity. When life brings loss, betrayal, heartbreak, and despair, we can call upon Kali to support us. She will shake up our personal narrative and burn away our egoic attachments. Her mythic energy is like a blazing fire—a place where we release our deepest wounds and offer our greatest desires in sacred ritual. In the name of wild transformation, Kali can pull out the harmful energies and simultaneously recalibrate our energy body and mind with potent healing.

Kali enables us to work with duality. Thanks to her we can stay steady inside the spectrum of love to hatred, joy to pain, life to death, vitality to suffering, abundance to loss, passion to emptiness. She encourages us to ride the edges of these emotional events and life happenings so that we may delve into the greater mysteries of life. We can create, deconstruct, and begin again. When we give ourselves permission to ignite our inner Kali, we shed lifetimes of fear and shame. By doing so we create opportunities to inspire others to do the same.

The Huntress spirit dances wildly with Kali's mythology as we discover that life's great dualities are in fact one. We can discover how our inner fierceness is like a vast ocean of compassion inside the feminine frequency. When we understand what it means to be fierce, we stand strong in our power. Releasing control of outcomes and the need for external validation is key to Kali's embodiment. Holding the audacity to be wild, fierce, and authentically empowered is the healing balm inside the evolved frequency of feminine power. This is the leadership required now and for the future.

No longer fear failure. Shed all tendencies
to defend or dominate to prove your worth.
Be the visionary with pure inner strength.
Clear action, strong center, tender heart—
begin again in the spark of Kali's flame.

The Huntress Tool Kit: Strategies for an Empowered Life

Transforming Warrior Wounds into Courageous Wisdom

The Huntress gives you the tools you need to live true to your gifts and share them freely with the world. The task is to gather, craft, and feed your authenticity in a way that is healthy, steady, and sustainable. To embody both softness and strength inside each moment is key to the process. Each breath becomes an opportunity to exhale fear and overwhelm, each inhale a way to flow with a strong, steady grace. The masculine warrior mentality of forcing, bullying, and controlling only leads to burnout. The outmoded, colonial ways of climbing the corporate ladder to dominate and manipulate others to achieve success is not useful to the Huntress. The feminine frequency holds a vast power that includes personal accountability, listening with compassion, and seeing the bigger picture. No longer get sucked into the vortex of victimization; no longer abandon your own truth. Rather, see what matters most, how to focus, process, plan and execute in alignment with right action. Understand on a deep level that fear-based planning provides only short-term solutions, often the quick fixes lead to greater imbalances. Embrace the art of letting go of things that don't contribute to empowering your essence. Feel your own emotions bubbling to the surface as a wake-up call to tend to your own body–mind temple.

In this precise moment, draw your awareness in and get curious about the deeper message or material wanting to be expressed. This ongoing inquiry can reprogram the mind from fear into courage. Questions like this become your living tool kit . . . "How can these imbalances, hardships, and challenges allow me to understand what the deeper lesson is? How can I redirect my energy to sculpt them into courageous wisdom and right action?"

No longer repress what you know and feel—or make excuses for what is wanting to be expressed. Like a clear channel of energy, express what is true and ask for support from your team when needed. Listen to the call of your own evolving nature daily. Develop a deep trust inside the extraordinary and intuitive realms that surround you. Welcome daily epiphanies and divine timings with curiosity. Trust, they have arrived for a reason. It takes courage to rise above the ordinary of everyday life. Embrace your intuitive insights as the sacred fuel that feeds each cycle and mission in your life.

Personal Attunement: Soul Care Is Gold

Daily acts of soul care are essential as a means to stay grounded in the body, clear in the mind, and expansive in your vision. No matter how busy you get, or what drama is going on in your life, it is vital to show up and commit to tending the fires of your personal needs. The effect is a steady, activated, purposeful life. When you feel good inside your body, you feel empowered. Every thought you have is received by your whole being. Your body becomes the storyteller, the living narrative of your lifetime. Get to know what physical practices light you up, and which practices allow you to relax and ground. Find the ways in which you can keep your mind spacious and inspired, and devote yourself to these wondrous rituals. These rhythms become a part of your support team. Physically you feel attuned. Mentally you clear toxic energies. Emotionally you feel how to channel positive energy. Spiritually you begin to feel a greater connection to self, community, and purpose. And you get an opportunity to explore your truest expression as you navigate your way through life.

Honoring Personal Process and Expressing Soul Gifts

Each one of us arrives at birth with a purpose, a calling in this present life, and karma from past lives to be worked through. Once this is acknowledged, the Huntress is no longer lonely or confused. Rather she becomes an expanded channel in service to soul visions and passions. This, in turn, becomes the antidote to the fear and inhibitions in daily life.

Reframing fear is how the Huntress sees from another perspective. The personal work involves getting out of our own way, committing to the task at hand, and releasing our tendency to take everything personally. We become more resourceful and resilient. When life changes direction, we can recover more quickly because we are grounded and connected to the pureness of our vision. We understand our own truth and we know how to express it to fortify the vision. The Huntress can share her spirit unapologetically with the world because she intimately understands that compassion is the key to clear vision and leadership. Simultaneously, she can support others to do the same. When there are opposing views, the practice of compassionate listening generates a non-defensive, non-competitive frequency. This is the gift of the embodied Huntress in action.

As you evolve over the course of your life, so does your calling. When you are on the precipice of great change, you may feel unclear about what's before you. When you are transitioning from one cycle to the next, fear may surface to get your attention. To get to the heart of your inner Huntress during times of change, ask yourself: *"Is this fear moving me, or is this the excitement of my true passion? What is the inner message wanting to emerge, and can I be courageous enough to listen?"*

Once you get a pulse on this energy, the next inquiry involves honoring your personal process while taking courageous steps towards what matters most to you. This will be unique to you. How you approach this will be very different from others.

When you tap into the quietest places within your soul, it will speak freely. When you feel safe enough to dream, you open yourself to clues to the direction you need to take. When you nourish yourself with enough rest, good food, and practices that enhance physical health, you will be supported in your soul expression. However, if you are constantly following, consuming, and distracting yourself you ignore the calls and miss the clues. The Huntress then loses her way on the path towards self-fulfillment. Her scent leaves her, her hearing gets muddled, she can no longer see in the dark, her support systems become imbalanced. Her ecosystem dries up.

It takes courage to break this cycle. It begins by making a choice to wake up your warrior energy and let it evolve into a wild, untamed, and powerful feminine enigma. You plant your seeds, water them with care, presence, and commitment. You show up with courage to witness their evolution. With peripheral visions intact, you intuit when to be tender and when to be fierce. And you continue to walk the path of right action while tending any wounds of self-doubt, fear, criticisms, lack of hope or support. Take them to the fire to burn, wash your warrior body clean in the river, and begin again. What tethers the Huntress to her vision is the commitment to express herself freely, wildly, and trust that her cause is worthy of this work.

> *"Some people say I was very brave,*
> *but I just didn't know any better.*
> *All I had was my originality."*
>
> **Buffy Sainte-Marie**

Building Stamina: Being Wildly You

We have all experienced those passages in life that feel dry, foggy, lackluster. We feel lost, without purpose or direction. When we experience loss, hardship, a mid-life reckoning or major life change, it can feel like a dark night of the soul. At these times you cannot see through the trees. You may barely get out of bed, let alone care for yourself or others. You lack any motivation to change. Can you remember a time in your life when you felt powerless or like your self-esteem had been crushed? What eventually allowed you to crawl out of this state?

Visualize the Huntress archetype before you. If you were to see her face, her clothing, her essence, what does that look and feel like? Visualizing the Huntress in this way, as part of your everyday support team, will be deeply supportive for the rest of your life. As you build stamina in your life, you are generating the inner strength of the Huntress. She is here to encourage you to be *wildly you*. You now have permission to live, breath, feel, express, and connect with your most radical, authentic nature. She arrives when you begin to doubt yourself, when fear takes over and begins to rule your decisions. The Huntress holds the dynamic power to set the boundaries you need to thrive in all areas of your life. And she reminds you that your boundaries need to shift as you evolve your body of work and meet what matters most to you in this cycle of life. At times she needs to soften to rejuvenate. Other times she is here to push you forward into the great unknown. She guides you to attune to mystery, magic, and divine timing.

No longer fear how your vision, purpose, and activation evolves throughout your life. You get to live out your life—not for anyone else, not to please, or prove, or play it safe. Take the big life questions like "who am I?" and listen. Receive the stirrings, the whispers, the awakenings at 3:00 a.m. Gather the resources and activate this information like the Huntress honoring her soul vision inside this great mystery of life.

The Huntress Invitation: Mindful Activation for Clear Vision

The Huntress invitation is to be in ongoing conversation with your inner dialogue and your environment. To become present to which daily fires you are tending. Observe when you are feeding lower energies of greed, guilt, or righteousness. Can you expand your listening skills to be truly present? Rather than listening only to figure out your response, enter the world of the one you are listening to and elevate them with your presence. This way of listening requires patience and the willingness to put your own agenda aside. It is most challenging when you are under stress, trying to get kids off to school, attempting to stay open to your partner's process, and when grief or life's great challenges are before us. The practice of presence and steadiness allows for greater clarity, connection, and balance in your relationship to self and others.

At some point in your life, you may have learned strategies from others that keep you from engaging on a deeper level. In this way you avoid intimacy. Observe when you tune out, and when a repetitive thought pattern takes over. This is a three-step process. First, acknowledge that you are no longer present—awareness is everything. Second, take a deep breath. Third, soften and let go of any judgements you have, whether of yourself or others. Now you begin again with an awakened presence. This is a practice that you will do over and over again, each time deepening your personal process and expanding your awareness. Whatever your chosen life path is, doing this will naturally improve the quality of what you put out into the world. Be it creativity, activism, leadership, business, or justice—your persona will exude compassion as an active listener, an engaged, kind, and respectful individual.

As the one thing we can count on in life is change, we can continue to hold the flame of our personal evolution.

Meditation

Visualize a large outdoor fire before you. This is a ceremonial fire where all your beloved soul friends and family are gathered. They are here in your honor; you are loved and supported. Your soul family is also here to honor your gifts and talents, the ways in which you contribute to the world—not necessarily related to your productivity or your career. This is a deeper ritual where your soul is given permission to be wholly expressed. There is no need to hide behind a role or to fear being abandoned, rejected, or shamed. This circle of community is here to hold you up and unconditionally support your visions.

Instead of seeing what is not working or what you aren't doing, see all the things that *are* working in your life. Feed this sacred fire with the Huntress vision that empowers you at the core of your being to live the life you are worthy of.

If the Huntress is ignored, ungrounded, and living in chaos, she will collapse and feel defeated. Anger, shame, and fear will shoot arrows of hardship and resentment into those she loves. She will veer off the natural trajectory of her life. Yet the wake-up call of the Huntress comes in the precise moment where we lose faith and ignore those deep inner stirrings. Can you imagine meeting those stirrings with curiosity and compassion? How would this look and feel for you personally?

Weaving in a daily gratitude practice is generative of transforming negativity into positivity. Meeting your inner ecosystem through journaling, conversation with trusted friends, and conscious mind–body practices bridge from lack to wholeness. You can transform your state quickly when you show up daily. Committing to what personally lights you up is key.

When you can no longer access joy or wonder, that is the Huntress calling you to come home to recalibrate. This is the time to gather your tools, name your resources, and practice compassion, goodness, and right actions. Your daily self-care boosts mind–body radiance. Catching the Huntress visions will come like glimmers of what is ready to birth through you and expand out into the world. The sacred hunt comes alive.

One direct way to listen, feed, and express the Huntress within is to ask this simple question: *"Does this path expand me, or make me complacent in my own life?"*

Answer the call to be fully present on this soul-reviving journey.
Each cycle, experience, thought, feeling, and action is part of
your universal metamorphosis. No longer fear the dark of the
mundane, look up to see the shimmery night sky. You are of ancient
composition. Be a child of the earth, witness her miraculous ways.
Ignite your torch and let it guide you into the world.
Love is the nectar inside the vision of the Huntress.

The Huntress Matrix

The Huntress holds the wisdom to evolve into your ensouled destiny. Sculptor, artist, mother, daughter, hunter, gatherer, lover, sister, activist, spirited friend—this path of service rides the tender and the tough in all of life's energy. At any given moment, she is willing to dive into the unknown and to acknowledge fear. She intuits the path of action that feeds her deepest purpose. Finding those sacred mirrors in which she can be vulnerable and share her deepest fears and greatest visions is the bravest work she can do. Honoring the big questions Who am I? Why am I here now? Where is the most valuable place to put my focus? How can I align to evolve into the karmic unfolding of self and greet the planetary shifts already in motion?

With inquiry and a connected body–mind system, her awakened sensory alertness guides her towards right action, goodness for all, and truth. The Huntress can see through the eyes of the artist, touch with the hands of a healer, and source filaments of the sacred while living with an awakened presence to all experiences. She can perceive and move energy within pain and struggle in herself and others, using this as an alchemical force to attain freedom. She understands that to get free from the narrative of the past is the greatest healing.

Staying present and steady inside the battles with self, the Huntress listens. Her quiver, arrows, and bow are at the ready. The owl is her protectress, encouraging false beliefs to fall away so her true nature may shine. Her vision extends over the whole landscape—she sees the big picture and understands where her healing energy is most needed.

No longer does she go onto the battlefield to prove herself right or to please others. Rather, her humble, fierce yet crystal-clear nature trusts that by gathering her resources, she will receive the wisdom needed to speak her truth, to stand tall for what she believes in. Trusting her inner spark, she no longer needs to hide or quiet her intelligence in fear of being rejected. The embodied Huntress gathers the kindred souls that see her true power and accept her for who she is, not for who she is not. Her sun-kissed arrow goes directly where she wants it to go. Her sword is a torch that encourages us to be wild, unbound, creative, messy, direct, and compassionate. Her craft is to channel her words, thoughts, emotions, and creations to evoke free will and justice inside the physical and spiritual planes. Connect with her daily, breathe your prayers into your inner Huntress. She is ready to listen, support, and co-create with you on your current journey.

The sequence of life's karmic unfolding becomes the fuel
to feed your personal evolution.
A choreographed dream flashes before you: tools are given,
resources are gathered, missions are explained.
With opulent synchronicity the support team
arrives on your doorstep.
No longer can you ignore the call.
Divine timing is on your side.

The Huntress ignites, moonstones stream from her mouth,
her unapologetic presence quickens within you.
Feed the fire of your visions, this in turn becomes the lifeline
that shapes your soul purpose.
Make art, build structures, grow food, guide others,
love with unbreakable devotion.
Permission is granted to enliven this earth
with your wildest creations.
No longer covet your skills or fear the judges,
or loneliness, or failure.

Pour your faith into freeing the dragons that hold you back.
In the quiet of the dark's stillness,
what is it that matters to you most?
What longs to be expressed through you?
Quiver to bow, arrows of your destined life's work
can no longer wait.

Now is the time, this one precious,
empowered and impassioned life awaits you!

Practices for Embodying the Huntress

~

Guided Visualization: Igniting the Huntress Within—Transforming Fear to Empower Your Energy Field

Take a pause to breathe fully in and breathe out. Do that again—maybe a sigh, a yawn, or a release in your gut. Imagine any armor over your body to slide off you. Become spacious like the sunset in your vision field. Let go of your agenda completely.

Now bring your attention to what you are fearful of or worried about.

What currently plays on repeat in your mind? What are the feelings or places that feel stuck inside your body? Where is your body holding excess or unresolved energy right now?

These energies are asking for your attention. Visualize them as layer upon layer of clothing, or like scarves covering your body. This may feel heavy or weighted. You may see colors, or memories may come to mind. Continue to surrender to this experience, breathing fully, softening your skin.

Visualize yourself gathering wood to ignite a blazing fire. This is a healing fire. Welcome any of your supporting guides, teachers, or soul friends to be in sacred ceremony with you. What does the landscape look like, are there any animals there to support you? As you feel ready to release the weight of your fears, any past experiences of pain, trauma, grief, or hardship, offer them to the fire. It may happen quickly, or you may need more time. As you watch these layers burn—be they physical, emotional, karmic, or spiritual—trust in the power of clearing your energy field for renewal.

Go further now, sifting and sorting what feels tired and unwanted within. Give this energy permission to leave your body. Is there anything else that may be holding you back from expressing your true gifts? Be curious about what is driving you. Perhaps your ego is running the show, based on strategies that may not be pure. Whatever it is, name it and offer it to the fire. Detach yourself from this narrative. It is no longer needed.

Trust this recalibration. Feel it in every cell of your body. Welcome this release and honor the truth of your healing in mind, body, and spirit. Sense the compassionate energy that is supporting you in this fire-cleansing ritual. Welcome this in. Bring this energy into your mind now. Allow your mind to become spacious, crystal clear, and listen for a message that may want to come through you. The Huntress is here now, supporting you to manifest the life you are worthy of. Your soul's calling has arrived within you.

Visualize the Huntress. Welcome her into the center of your body. She has arrived to reclaim your power and your truth. She will support you as you navigate your healing journey. Connect with her energy, and trust that you can ignite the flame of her warrior spirit within you as needed.

Come back to your body, focusing on your breath. Feel the Earth underneath you and sense the vast sky above. Thank yourself for inviting the Huntress strength and vision into you.

Journal about your experience, observe how you feel.

The Huntress Expansion: An Invocation

Answer the call to be a courage expander, vision generator,
and peace activist with your soul.
Become the lighthouse in stormy waters.
Take risks in the name of pursuing your vision.
Shape-shift your anger into passion.
Pay the good faith forward, it takes courage to hear the call.
No longer fear falling or making mistakes—
you will rise again, and wiser indeed.
Forgiveness is the secret weapon and the pure healer
of all times.

Be willing to stand tall for the causes you can no longer ignore.
Service is an act of love; humility is more potent than winning.
In-source before you out-source.
Trust in the power of change.
You are evolving into the best version of you
every step of the way.

Fill your chalice with present-moment truths.
As fear arises, feed it to the fire, witness its evolution.
Cast prayers freely, affirm boundaries,
and no longer covet your true power.
Trust in your Huntress's mission
to express her soul gifts in the world.
In return receive the luminous arrows of worthiness,
love, and courage—the flame
of your inner vision ignites.
No longer forgotten, divinely remembered.

Breathwork to Ignite Inner Power

Intention
To inhabit your true source of power.

Light a candle, find a comfortable seat. This can also be done outside in the sun.

Place one hand on your solar plexus, and one hand on your lower abdomen.

Find your rooted connection to the earth, streaming like an anchor from your solar plexus down to the earth below.

Welcome your rising nature, extending your spine through the crown of your head towards the sky.

Inhale for six counts in through the nose, hold the breath for six, and exhale for six out the mouth making a hissing sound as if you are fogging up a mirror.

Repeat six times.

With each breath and hold, visualize the flame of fire growing steadily within you.

Locate where fear, confusion or imbalance lives in your body, and give it permission to burn away.

Merge with the colors and shapes of the flame and welcome it as a connection to your inner source and power.

Begin a rapid-fire breath: focusing on the exhale, draw your navel and solar plexus towards your spine as quickly and steadily as you can.

Try three rounds, eventually getting up to 40 rapid-fire breaths per round. Find a soft pause in between the rounds. Visualize your inner Huntress coming alive—clear, powerful, and connected to her own source.

Sit in silence for two minutes to integrate any sensations or messages that the Huntress may have for you.

A Huntress Visioning Practice:
Embracing Authenticity, Activating Creativity

Light a candle.

Sit in quiet contemplation or meditation for five minutes.

Practice letting go of expectations on the exhale, and welcome in clear and renewed energy on the inhale.

Visualize your embodied Huntress before you. She is here to remind you of your authenticity and core power. She dissolves defensiveness and reminds you to peel away the layers of control and toxic egoic identities. She is the face of creative destruction.

She has come with tools and resources to support your evolving Huntress spirit.

What tools, resources, sentiments, and actions does she offer you? Is there a word that will anchor you into your true self?

Create a poem, an affirmation or a sentence that includes your word and the tools provided.

This can be followed by daily practices that support you or projects/creations that the Huntress in you is ready to activate and embody.

Share your vision with a friend and place it on your vision board.

Fear Tracking: A Free-Write Practice to Empower Your True Power

Name the fears and worries that are currently occupying space in your mind.

Track the origin of these fears: Are they inherited belief systems from family or culture? Or manifestations from your current situation?

Locate where fear lives in your body, journal about its location, how it feels, what color or tone it manifests in your physical body. Receiving this information will allow you to recognize when fear takes you over so you can transform it more readily in the moment.

Journal about anger: When does it get provoked? How does it express itself? How are others affected by your anger?

In what way does fear hold you back from being fully engaged in life or limit the quality of your daily experience?

Journal the ways in which you can self-remedy your fears. For example, "When I get enough sleep and exercise, I am less fearful."

Or "When I journal my fears, I realize that they are not true; rather they rule my thoughts and overshadow the way I can access my true strength."

Complete your tracking practice by creating a personal empowerment affirmation. Begin with "I am . . ." or "I will . . ."

Journal Prompts to Embrace the Huntress Within

Characteristics of the Embodied Huntress
Courageous | Devoted | Instinctual | Change-Maker
Adaptable | Resourceful

Where do you welcome the inner Huntress to guide you?

What are you currently wanting to cultivate and express in your life?

Describe the ways in which you can fuel your authenticity to share your visions unapologetically with the world.

How do you support others in your life to do the same?

Journal about what expands you, empowers you, and ignites your inner passions to come alive.

What matters to you most right now?

How do you welcome your inner Huntress to join you in expanding a full, meaningful, and connected life?

Journal Prompts to Transform the Huntress's Shadow

Characteristics of the Huntress in Her Shadow
Disempowered | Fearful | Defensive
Reactive | Frustrated | Dramatic

Name ways you project your fears onto your future. Describe situations in which your mind goes to the worst-case scenario.

Do you experience shame in your life? If so, write about where, why, and track its origin.

Journal the mind chatter that starts with the "I am never . . . I am always . . . this always happens to me."

Now, reframe those sentences into empowering phrases. Connect to what is true in the moment and let go of the constant negativity in your mind.

Clear Vision, Courageous Heart

Resilient beyond measure,
the Huntress spirit is equally strong and soft.
Compassion fuels intuition.
Boundaries affirm presence.

Anchoring into earth, I rise with the fire of the morning sun.
Dancing with the whispering winds, I surrender to the unknown.
In that moment I give it all to the majestic starry night sky.
An electricity of unfurling depth spirals out of me.
There is a death of my old self, like a trail of tears behind me.
No longer defined by fear or fight, I gaze across the horizon.
Unknown future, sovereign at last
from the narrative that wasn't even mine.

This yellow surge of life poured out of my lungs
like mammoth sunflowers.
Honeybees, dancing trees. The wild ocean stirs my mind pure.
Ready to give each moment the attention it deserves.
I stand for and embody this luminous Huntress vision.
Free to finally be comfortable in this body-life skin.
Each moment worthy of gracious attention.

Here my sword of truth, there the shield of compassion.
My strategic, wildly intuitive heart—mind evolves
into freedom for all living beings.

The Lover

"Love rests on two pillars: surrender and autonomy.
Our need for togetherness exists alongside our need for separateness."

Esther Perel

Who Is the Lover?

The Lover understands that self-awareness is her superpower inside any relationship. Her boundaries are clear, either refined or porous as needed. She is wild at heart and stays true to her mission: to source the pure frequency of love while going as deep into the realms of intimacy as possible in this lifetime. She holds nothing back. She wears her heart on her sleeve, in her womb, on her breasts, in her mind, and in her eyes. She walks her body to the acceptance temple daily, adorns to please herself first. Her mind is quick to discern when attachments to past or future cloud her vision of love. She remembers, redirects, and returns to the source of love deep within.

When grief arrives, she embraces the sensations, then retreats and allows the salt of her tears to bless the earth. The Lover has a kindred union with grief, for she understands that it is another form of love. She knows that her grief needs to be fully embraced, listened to, felt, witnessed, and loved. This is how it moves through her, healing. Personal and collective attachments peel away and dissolve into the abyss of life's great mysteries. The Lover returns to the acceptance temple, naming her truth, reclaiming what she loves.

The act of creation is love in motion. Creative pursuits amplify the love channels within, while clearing imbalanced emotions. We get into the artist's zone, and all else falls away. When attachments are released, egoic ways are dissolved. We can see through our own shadows, feelings of aloneness and disconnection begin to merge with the energy field of love. A true self-love evolves as we grow and change throughout our lives—if we accept the invitation. The task is to accept these shifts and greet our own spirit with permission to love the good, the bad, and the ugly. It takes courage and discipline to embrace ourselves through the whirlwind times and the down times. The questions arise: *"How do I love today?"* and *"How is my love being expressed through me—into others and out into the world?"*

This brings us to the tender and steady strength of the feminine Lover. She can see beyond the romanticized love of teenage crushes, beyond the material, superficial, people-pleasing kind of love. She goes deep into her own well of compassion to source her love. She practices forgiveness when appropriate and no longer takes her inner child wounds into her relationships.

Love as the Ultimate Resource: The Invitation Awaits

The power of love is timeless. One of the sacred tasks in our lifetime is to love with and from freedom. Love is the life-gate towards living with sovereignty. Yet its energetic frequency becomes fragmented by the complexities of human nature.

An invitation into the limitless field of love awaits you. It begins with you. Become an expander of love. Offer it first and this ultimate resource will magnetize every thought, experience, and perception in your life. The receptive channels of love become vast and wildly attractive when you surrender your attachments to how love is supposed to save you.

Understanding how love flows in your life and what blocks you from feeling love will support you to embody the Lover archetype. If you want to transform your life, begin with love as the ultimate resource. Being present to your self-care regime, getting enough sleep, spending time in nature, and igniting your creative channels will increase the organic flow of love. Understand how negative self-talk, addiction, jealously, comparison, staying in unhealthy relationships and turning away from what brings you joy block the flow of passion and possibility. And as with the law of attraction, this disturbed frequency then magnetizes other lower energies.

To infuse more consciousness into your love journey begin to track the flow of loving and joyous energy in your body. What does that feel like? Connect to the sensations, thoughts and behaviors that follow. Observe what restricts the flow of positive energy in your life. Take it on as a personal responsibility to activate the practices and conditions that open your body, mind, and heart. Once you initiate this kind of self-awareness, you will understand more clearly how and why you choose to turn away from love. Then you will return to your center and discover the clarity that comes from accepting to choose love and compassion over fear and judgement.

Undertaking the work of the heart is a profound commitment. Allow the act of surrender to be unique to each moment and experience in life. Thus, a softening process matures, and present-moment awareness amplifies. You build your positive love reserves so that they flow in and out with ease. You no longer get derailed by every disturbing comment or action, rather you stand in the compassionate matrix of the feminine Lover. An unwavering self-acceptance naturally generates unconditional self-love. The inner critic transforms into the Lover within. And when thoughts, feelings, and actions become burdened by the load of lack and fear once again, you will have the self-awareness to inquire and reroute towards compassion. The connected Lover accepts the invitation to make peace with the natural ebb and flow of love in her ecosphere. Like giving birth, the contractions and expansions eventually usher her divine creations into manifestation. Trusting in this organic journey, she fills the well of her soul to the brim and accepts love as her ultimate, most precious resource.

The work is to begin, end, and return to love as the essential gate towards a joyous, fulfilled existence.

"When we protect ourselves, so we won't feel pain,
that protection becomes like armor, like armor that imprisons
the softness of the heart."
Pema Chodron

The Lover Lost in the Shadows

The Lover lost in the shadows is ruled by her attachment to past wounds and previous relationships. She lacks self-awareness and has an unresolved desire to be ruled by scarcity. She believes there will never be enough love in herself. She feels unworthy of true love from others. She lives her life half empty, never having enough time, money, or love to live the life she wants. She lives in a constant state of comparison. She seeks drama in all forms—in her workplace, at home, and in her relationships. These are the ways in which she pushes intimacy and deeper expressions of love out of her life. She fears intimacy and the drama acts as a distraction to her own healing. She avoids turning inward to see, feel, and listen; she avoids the inner work that is essential to her own liberation. By living in the shadow, the lost and disembodied Lover recycles habitual patterns that trigger and feed her core wounds. This is how she pushes love away and continues to live in the pain of unresolved or repressed trauma from the past.

Image obsession steals our personal power. We become players in this patriarchal and conforming paradigm, sometimes without even realizing it. We place more focus on the way we want to look or be perceived and avoid how we want to feel. In time, this gripping control of our external appearance drives the need for more outside validation and leaves us bypassing our self-worth. We deplete our own reserves, our well runs dry, and we lose sight of the pure self-love that ignites our spirit. Our self-esteem becomes fragile, and we end up spiraling through the same kind of abandonment or pain we may have experienced in the past.

Emotional and sexual abuse may have triggered the Lover into a state of freeze, fight, or flight. With a fragile and fractured self-esteem, we question our worthiness and abandon our gut instincts. We harden, freeze, and deflect the flow of pure love—we don't trust it. The Lover's deepest work is to de-armor our heart and liberate our sexuality by reclaiming self-love.

Attachments and old stories block our perception of love. They come from the past and form specific desires to have things look or feel a certain way. This creates an illusion or perception of something other than the love that is present to us in the moment. Understanding that we have the power to choose which frequency of love we tune into is to source love at its purest distillation.

The residue of past pain and unresolved trauma, both personally and collectively, provokes the desire to control our environment. The narratives of our past complicate our relationship to self and others. By tracing the origin of specific triggers and patterns, we can develop compassion, practice forgiveness, and understand ourselves more fully. This is emotional maturity in action.

To reclaim the pure, distilled essence we were born with is to practice unconditional self-love. We get to choose how we show up and love ourselves first. No one else can do this work. No lover can come in to fix our broken pieces. The work is to understand how we become triggered and fall into blame or shame and how this affects our perception of self-love. Do we react by turning away, running, leaving, and retreating to self-loathing? Once we begin peeling the layers of armor off our heart, we begin to feel our entire system shift. We feel connected to our truth and closer to accessing what lights us up.

On a global level, we can see how sexism, agism, racism, patriarchy, homophobia, environmental imbalance, and non-inclusivity trigger low self-esteem, anger, and sadness. We can begin to understand how those outdated, imbalanced paradigms have existed to control freedom and push us out of love and care for one another. The work of the embodied feminine Lover is to catch ourselves feeding these repressed ways of living and to rise above them. Getting to know, listen, and love our own bodies and trust the sensations that arrive in the moment is essential to our healing.

We can step into leadership through the intelligent, compassionate heart; this is the wild-hearted, awakened feminine power of love.

Working through Unresolved Pain to Access Deep Healing

To liberate the Lover within, it's essential to work through grief, trauma, and pain from our childhood through to the present day. When we push down unresolved grief and pain, we block our capacity to heal. When we begin to unravel the hidden emotions within, give them a voice, and name them, we unlock the ways in which we attempt to avoid our pain. By understanding how our hurts are affecting us, we slowly open to deeper intimacy.

To allow difficult emotions to move through you and not rule you helps you mature emotionally. Such emotions may come in the form of rage, anger, sadness, or anxiety. The task is to pause, listen, and find a safe way to work through the emotions. The emotion needs to be expressed as you acknowledge that your intuitive self is sharing very important information with you.

The journey of healing from sexual shame and trauma is an essential undertaking. It takes courage to seek the support needed and begin the process. It will get messy, and memories will be re-lived. Finding safe spaces to share your story and experience personal healing is the Lover's work. You are worthy and deserving of a revolutionary kind of self-love. You deserve to respect yourself and radically accept your process as a compassionate work in progress. When our self-care regime is harmonized, we will be able to see more clearly where addictions, emotional blocks, and lack of self-esteem surfaces.

The healing work you commit to daily will guide you to the self-acceptance temple. There you will mend the old wounds, reclaim unconditional compassion, learn forgiveness for self and others. This self-acceptance journey begins and ends with how ready you are to commit to loving yourself. Every day is an opportunity to begin again.

"True forgiveness is when you can say,
'Thank you for that experience.'"
Oprah Winfrey

The Power of Forgiveness:
Living with Compassion

Forgiveness not only accelerates our own healing, but it propels us to the next stage of our emotional and intuitive maturity. To forgive is not to dismiss or erase the events that caused us pain, rather it is to enhance the quality of our life. Our current joys and our future freedoms are tethered to how we resolve our past. Each life experience that requires the power of forgiveness is a unique gift in disguise. We need time to heal. Once we can trust our inner reckonings and understand how to come to peace inside our personal pain and loss we will know when we are ready to move forward. With conscious self-awareness we can forgive those we believe to have caused us pain. We let go of blaming and judging; in this way we activate our own healing. When we take the blame off others, we can begin to create space to feel our own pain.

Even more important than forgiving others is forgiving ourselves. This kind of profound forgiveness brings peace, as we honor each life cycle as the valuable material in which we build resilience and engage in personal inquiry. In these pivotal, life-altering moments, the awakened heart washes us clean and our perception of who we are shifts. We accept our own imperfections. The striving towards perfection begins to morph. Lack, fear, and the pillars of self-loathing crumble. Miraculously we accept and love others more deeply for who they are, not who we want them to be. We can see their true gifts, and in doing so, recognize our own.

Being present with our habitual thought patterns and our daily actions is how we begin our self-forgiveness journey.

There are two choices inside any situation. One way is to hang on, take things personally, deflect our pain onto others, feel resentful, angry, and unfulfilled by our actions and choices. Another way is to soften, release the defensive, critical and judgemental reactions and become finely attuned to what is true in the moment. Each moment in life is worthy of authenticity.

When you loosen your grip on attempting to control every aspect of life, you encourage forgiveness and compassion to be your guides. You let down the armor around your heart and feel more alive, connected to each present moment. The practice of self-forgiveness gives us permission to rest when we need to and turn within when we feel overwhelmed. Self-forgiveness motivates you to practice soul-care in ways you haven't before. Let it begin with intentional rest and conscious activation. Resist the temptation to engage in fragmented, diluted, and disempowered narratives. When the authentic desire to forgive others arrives, make it sacred and follow this path up spirit mountain to release your pain in the name of freedom for all.

Find healing in how you create and what you intend, speak and vision. Naturally this sacred formula will bring forth your divine will. Your intuition sparks in the most unexpected ways. Be prepared to listen.

Trust in your goodness; love yourself wild and free. Be heart-struck by the beauty of the simplest things. Change begins by returning to a soft, nourishing, and peaceful kind of self-love. Your devotion to the goodness in all of life will bring revolutionary transformation. With devotion, be guided by compassion and forgiveness. No longer doubt your capacity to love free of conditions. Give thanks for the lessons learned and trust in your resilience. Prayerfully and with reverence, honor the ways in which you see, feel, hear, taste, and touch this gift of life with a heart full of compassion.

Love is infinite. When we overcome the mentality of lack and scarcity, we merge with the immeasurable essence of love. Make this kind of loving a daily practice. It will generate a spiritual, vastly intimate, deeply vulnerable, and exquisite sanctuary within you. By synergizing with love as the source of true joy and fulfillment, we trust that hardships will eventually dissolve. At every crossroads, every twist and turn of life, an endless sea of love patiently awaits you.

Embodied Self-Love as the Baseline

The Lover is symbolic of the vital life force energy that births the world alive. She seeks deep forms of intimacy while living a sensual and joyful existence. The Lover exudes magnetic energy and does not hold back on freedom of expression. She surrounds herself in beauty and creativity. Sourcing love, light, and passion is her mission; this authentic *joie de vivre* is built upon an unwavering, endless sea of goodness. Her thirst for going deeper into the channels of love is quenched by her devotion to loving herself through all stages and cycles of life. When she falls off her center, she regains balance through self-forgiveness. Once again, she purifies her heart temple, cleanses her vision, and shares her wisdom with the world.

The Lover archetype draws within to self-nourish before extending her energy back out into the world. She understands how energy flows in both directions—in and out. She trusts the fallow times that allow her to quietly rebuild her vision. And in times of chaos, she does not get swept away in the drama, she knows tomorrow will be different. With love as her baseline, she drinks from the nectar of life's miraculous beauty. The Lover's devotion to sourcing compassion from her core evokes dimensional elegance in her every step.

The Lover abides by an unwavering regime of self-love and soul care. Such inspiration comes from the desire to feel clear, bright, and embodied. Her radiant inner beauty organically alchemizes into the external. The Lover glows throughout her lifetime; she is not afraid of aging, rather she welcomes the changes as wisdom rites. Her self-care begins with rest; if there isn't enough sleep, the body can't heal or regain its flow. She recognizes what triggers the cycles of unease in her life, and she is aware that intensity, restlessness, or negativity brings the body into a further state of distress. When needed, the Lover seeks counsel and support from healers for mind and body. Because she has committed to unconditional listening and loving, she does not turn away; rather she leans into the healing that is knocking on her door.

The Lover creates space for mindfulness practices such as meditation, be it sitting, walking, or sacred movement. Her creative pursuits—painting, writing poetry, gardening, dancing, cooking, and handicrafts—keep her mind channels bright and her heart aglow. The Lover is so connected to her body that when it speaks to her she pauses and listens. Intuitive messaging comes to her through her body; this body talk becomes more powerful than the lower frequencies of the egoic mind. This relationship with her body temple is unique and deeply satisfying. It builds an authentic resilience that radiates to all she meets. Like the hummingbird, she is the dancer of intimacy who can awaken the heart song inside the wildflowers.

Your Body, Your Temple: Revolutionary Self-Acceptance

Through all the mysterious cycles of life, one thing remains essential: the Lover honors her body as her most sacred temple. As her physical body naturally transforms, she nourishes herself with the nectar it deserves. The Lover's relationship to her body is an ongoing practice of deep intimacy. When the body speaks, she listens. There is an unshakeable trust she has formed through her practice of self-love, and she receives the messages for recalibration, forgiveness, and compassion as they arrive. Adjusting her daily intake of food and energy as needed, she nourishes herself the way she would her own child. Not over or under indulging, she seeks balance with food to harmonize her sacred vessel. When energetically overwhelmed, she creates time to rest, if only for five minutes of lying down to replenish. Plant medicines fortify her evolving heart vision. Caring for others—animals, children or elders—warms her heart. She seeks support when her body speaks of another healing ready to move through her.

Our capitalist, patriarchal, and media-driven culture advocates for slim, voluptuous female bodies—more of this, less of that, implants, enhancements, Botox, fad diets. The desired body type becomes a seed implanted from a young age. If you grew up in a culture or family that praised one body type over another, you are most likely affected by these images, which in turn transform into thoughts, patterns, and behaviors.

Begin by understanding your attitude to body image. Pay attention to the impulse to control food and the desire to constantly present yourself externally (by abandoning your inner power). Healing comes through understanding how body image affected your childhood, adolescence, young adulthood, to where you are now in life. Your family of origin or chosen communities may have left you hungry for more approval, attention, and acknowledgement. Once this is understood, and held with compassion and forgiveness, the ability to accept and truly love your body begins.

What would it feel like if you could love every part of your body, even the parts you once saw as imperfect? You may not have been raised to love and care for yourself as the first step on the essential path towards fulfillment. Yet we are all born into this world with a sacred task to complete. What would it feel like to call that kind of daily love forward? Can you imagine beginning and ending your day with a loving awareness towards yourself, even on the hard days? Become a love huntress in life—be it giving or receiving—by inviting in a deeper intimacy with all forms of life. Surprisingly, the armor around your heart falls away and the constant flurry of judgements dissolves. Your way of living becomes guided by the power of love.

Practicing self-acceptance is essential to personal evolution. You get to become your own love guru and tap into the divine source of creation. Life itself is a wondrous, revolutionary blessing! It lives inside this moment as you breathe in and out. The birth of a new day, the death of the day passed. The emergence of the glorious sunrise, the starry night sky expressing its own majesty. And we begin again inside this holy vessel of our own hearts beating, reminding us that we too are of this origin that is love. We are creators of love—ready and willing to swim with its changing tides and soar through the skies with our wings unfurled.

The initiation begins by loving and accepting every ounce of your body. This love revolution will not only heal you but will ripple far and wide. It will evolve the feminine frequency to embody a sovereign, compassionate, and powerful leadership across the planet.

Infuse your heart's consciousness with the primordial rhythms sourced in the womb of Mother Earth. Merge with the shifting dimensions of the elements. Be humbled by the complexity of nature's choreographic symphony. Movement feeds evolution, silence nourishes darkness—as the light returns, a new cycle begins. Freedom awaits you inside this archetypal dance of life. Train your eye to see beauty inside the pain. Be with those who have endured loss and are grieving. Sink your spiritual heart into the sea of bottomless compassion. The flower of your heart blooms when you no longer define its edges. Let your love be limitless.

Beyond Roles and Attachments: Love as the Source of Bliss

Discovering love as the source of bliss is often initiated through our relationship to others. It may be formed in childhood through our caregivers, and later sparked by the innocence of our first crush. We begin to form roles and identities inside our love languages and expressions. We may take on specific roles without even being conscious of them. The caregiver, the nurturer, the provider, and the problem solver are relationship archetypes within themselves. We seek meaningful relationships, and our impressions of what "love" means becomes embedded into our psyche.

As humans we are meaning-making machines. We play chess with life and love, most often based on moves in our past. Our experiences then become the stories by which we identify ourselves. However, this approach to love dwells in the surface realms of life. We play out inherited or adopted roles and box ourselves into fixed identities. These often leave us hungry for a more evolved, intimate, and universal kind of love. In any love relationship, when the initial romance settles is there still poetry that stirs the soul? What is your relationship to love beyond the crush stage? How do you let it evolve beyond the fairy tale romance? When we no longer project our unresolved personal work onto others, we can open our awareness and feel love as a unifying force that goes beyond the realm of relationships. This is the seed of liberation inside the field of love, and yours to be planted.

A deeper understanding of love requires a transcendence of fixed roles and identities. It's as if the roles that you play in your relationships or your career become so sculpted that they harden you. These fixed roles become barriers to your capacity to evolve beyond the hardships of the past. They limit your potential to transform the way you love. When you set yourself free from being "only this" or "just that" you generate space to grow. You return to the source of who you are—which is love.

Freeing yourself from fixed identities to source a fluid, universal essence of love requires conscious self-awareness. Be it as a daughter, sister, wife, lover, friend, mother, grandmother, professional, provider or caregiver, you generate personal and collective stories within each role. When imbalanced, you cope by overcompensating and limit your potential by playing the victim, martyr, or power-over roles. And when you don't live up to your own expectations, guilt, shame, blame, and repressed anger start to drive your thoughts and behaviors. Whether it's inherited or adopted, when you discover where you block your own sense of freedom inside the role, your ego becomes spacious. You generate a liberated, less dependent kind of love within.

To feed the fixed roles that your inner child perceived as the "pre-destined" life perpetuates a narrative that is static and essentially lifeless. Yet, as humans we are always evolving. Your relationship towards who you are and how you love also needs to evolve. There should be no limitations on how you manifest love in your life. To release the stories, roles, identities, and attachments is to generate love as the place you begin and end your days, and ultimately your life. The two largest events in existence are birth and death. The power of love lives inside each breath you take.

Imagine yourself free of predefined roles. Who are you now?
How do you see yourself? How do you feel love without these
roles? Connect to humanity and the ones who cross your path as
the soulful messengers to evolve both of you. Go beyond thinking
about what you get or don't get. Rather than thinking "I am in

this situation or relationship, and I have to make it work," tell yourself "This is an opportunity for growth, I will do the inner work with love for myself and others." Instantly the pressure you place on yourself and others falls away. There is more space to feel into what wants to come through.

The daily undertaking of the attuned Lover is to consciously understand when the ego controls, motivates, and manipulates. You begin to take things less personally and accept that everyone has work to do on how they love. You have more compassion. Self-love and self-awareness inside relationships is perhaps the deepest, most essential work to be done in your lifetime.

Over time, you become more conscious of the effect of your words and actions on others. You wake up and take responsibility for who you are and the effect you have on those around you. You become aware of where you place your attention, the way you choose to spend your days. You become the channel for how you want to live. This is the path towards wild-hearted living and loving. It takes devotion, grace, and an understanding that surrendering to what no longer serves is a daily undertaking.

This is your life to live, and the more you choose love, the more love will grow. You must be willing to let go of your old self in order to change how you generate love in your life. And when you feel hurt or angry and the desire to regress into your inner child presents itself, soften to feel the bodily sensations. Notice the thoughts that arise and the actions that want to come forward. Do not respond until you are calm. Take some deep breaths. Engage in mundane tasks, drink a glass of water, get some fresh air. Lean into the frequency of goodness.

Being in nature can help dissolve your attachment to roles or identities. Immersing yourself in the beauty and simplicity of nature, in the natural cycle of the seasons, allows you to be embraced by the wondrous source of life itself. Observing plant and animal life takes you out of seeing yourself as the center of the picture. It gives your ego the space to become less attached to your story. Dwelling in the mystery of the earth's cosmology brings surprise and awe into your energy field.

Nature becomes the quintessential force to free you of personal limitations, jaded perceptions, excess material desires and past wounds. The symbolic heart of the earth becomes an anchor point for our own physical and mental transformation. Love is a unifying force. The disparate parts of you are embraced by something larger, as if you are being held and taken care of. Trust in the human potential to be enveloped by a potent force of love that goes beyond theories and romantic sentiments. Give yourself fully to the dance of love; let it be a ceremonial journey. Let the winds of change replenish your vision and soften your heart. The boundless sky is waiting for your return.

Self-awareness is the key and a deep-seated self-love practice is the door to a loving, sovereign, and fulfilled life.

Mythic Muse: Oshun, Orisha Goddess of Love and Abundance

Oshun is the Orisha Goddess of love, abundance, healing, and fertility. The Orisha deities belong to the Yoruba religion, which has its roots in West Africa.

Oshun's power is steeped in a sensual, fierce, and revolutionary self-love. Her self-worth is built on her own terms: she does not seek validation or approval for her external appearance. She trusts her gut instincts. Her unwavering self-worth allows her to make crystal-clear boundaries without taking on guilt, shame, or blame. Oshun is neither the martyr nor the victim. She is the evocative feminine spark that generates abundance, balance, and the pure, infinite source of love inside every living energy on this planet.

As the Yoruba legend goes, the god of all gods, Olodumare, summoned the female deity Oshun to Earth to form a new world. She arrived dressed in a golden gown, her strikingly beautiful dark skin adorned with glistening jewels, flirtatious, free, and confident. Upon greeting the group of male deities with which she was to create the world, she was unimpressed by their ignorance and their inability to see her true gifts. Although they found her beauty alluring, they were aloof to her life-giving powers. They didn't think they needed Oshun to birth a new world.

Feeling unseen and unvalued, Oshun fled to the Moon where she bathed herself in the glow of her own elegance, wisdom, and beauty. Oshun's move to the Moon caused the Earth to dry up. There was no more water, no plant or animal life. The confused male deities returned to Olodumare for counsel and he observed Oshun's absence. He explained how Oshun's ability to generate love and beauty to spark the world alive was essential to creating a new world.

The male deities found Oshun and showered her with apologies and blessings, begging her return. They now understood that her life force was essential. Oshun accepted their apologies on the condition that they did not dismiss her power and wisdom again. Upon her return, the world instantly became lush, fertile, and filled with the most exquisite beauty—just like Oshun herself.

Work with Oshun to Reclaim Self-Love and Affirm Boundaries

Channel the power of Oshun's source of love and abundance when you feel disconnected from self-love. Embody her power when you find yourself suffering from worry, fear, or scarcity. Return to an empowered, embodied feminine love to manifest your dreams.

Call upon Oshun's exquisite force of nature and receive the radiant glow of the moon. Visualize her luscious dark skin, her shimmery robes, her shapely body adorned in jewels and gems. She adorns herself in the way that makes her feel sexy, sensual, erotic. She births each day by welcoming the power of authentic self-love. Everything she touches transforms into gold.

She understands that worry is like praying for the things you don't want to happen. When her instincts detect that the divine feminine way is not being honored or respected, she affirms her boundaries and strategizes her next mission. Her daily ritual is to discover the deepest forms of love. Her living prayer is to share the beauty and abundance of her world.

The Sovereign and Liberated Lover: Accessing Pure Intimacy

The Lover brings her desires into life through clear intention.

Inviting the sovereignty of our sexuality is to awaken the creative channels within. Therefore, it is worthy to pour our attention on healing and liberating our sexuality. When we are not hiding nor repressing our sacred sexuality, and when we can access safe spaces and trusted partners to explore our own Lover's awakening, we become empowered. We tap into a source of wildly creative energy steeped in bliss. We open to another level of unification within our own soul; that unification may also expand into our partners as well.

With a partner who can listen and be sensitive to our personal needs, we feel safe enough to express what turns us on and off. This goes beyond past images and experiences. Trusting, feeling, and knowing how to ask for what we want is the work. To delight in the divine act of sex is to tap into the source of creation itself. This is our birthright. We are deserving and worthy of being loved and adored in this way. We set the standards.

The Lover embodies pure erotic energy. This goes far beyond Western perception of the erotic, beyond pornographic images, beyond what is perceived as "sexy" in our culture. This erotic energy dwells in both psychic and physical space. It is both a spiritual eroticism and a wildly magnetic, mysterious, and pure physicality.

The embodied Lover can co-create in physical space while engaging in the psychic, intuitive, and spiritual realms. There is a creative and playful alchemy in the soul of the divine feminine Lover. She can tap into the *prana* or life force that lives inside the elements. She is the center of the flower, filled with pollen—ready and open to attract the right kind of bee or pollinator that will disseminate her love.

She gives love freely and receives love freely. Yet her emotional maturity allows her to discern where and when to give and receive that love. She understands when the love being given is unclean, manipulative, and conditional. She does not strive to be the pleaser, rather she listens to her natural impulses, feels the desire to create from within, and acts upon her instincts.

The Lover exudes openness, bliss, joy, freedom. This energy becomes so authentically radiant that it inspires everyone else to live with love, passion, and intimacy in this way. She holds nothing back. The seductive allure of pleasure and playfulness are not repressed, rather they are unbounded and clear. She is wholly dedicated to the highest essence of connection in both the physical and spiritual planes. This allows her to access deeper forms of intimacy within all her relationships.

Can we open to the act of finding our mates as a primal source of creation? This is the essence of *chi, shakti, prana*—the life force that fuels our passions and catalyzes them out in the world. Such passions—whether sexual passion or our creative passions such as art, music, dance, poetry—spark the Lover into life.

The feminine Lover inspires deep intimacy, radical self-love, sensuality, and a self-awareness that allows for open communication. She understands the law of attraction and directs her energy in both a refined and expanded capacity. When letting go and forgiveness are necessary to the process, she answers the call. Her finely-tuned channels keep her heart vision clear and clean. The embodied Lover seeks both depth and freedom in her relationships. She is wildly independent yet desires the kind of profound intimacy that breaks all rules. She goes beyond past limitations and stories of role-playing and societal paradigms. She pours her soul into what she loves and whom she loves. A magical, sensual allure gives her a radiance that inspires others to love tender and to dream big. She is the dancer of intimacy, the creatress of life force, and the divine feminine alchemy that lights up our world.

The Lover's Matrix

Let love become your baseline, the place you go back to in times of chaos and fear. When stress overcomes you, return to the essence of compassion. When self-loathing clouds your vision, practice forgiveness. When you feel empty, take your heart to spirit mountain, and find the treasures that await you. It takes courage to embrace every ounce of who you are. Be true to loving you.

Celebrate your wild side. Be sexy for you. Erotica lives in every living and breathing entity on this planet. Welcome pleasure on all levels. Give yourself yes days. Practice the art of saying no.

When life brings despair and loss, let your pain transform into prayers for the divine. Discover the edges of love and loss as part of the whole. Let this devotional act of love bring you to your knees. Name the blessings of being alive. This is love. These fleeting moments of pure bliss are worthy of your attention.

And when you look back in time you will see this as ecstasy in motion. May you courageously walk, breathe, and live in love until you transcend into love itself.

Generating the Frequency of Love: To Heal and Be in Service to the World

Whatever your love story is, trust that it can become an act of revolution. It takes courage to carry on in the wake of broken hearts, loved ones lost, tragic happenings, promises not honored, untruths told. And yet there is wisdom in the lived experience of loss. Every heartbreak deepens the Lover wisdom within.

Whatever storms you have weathered, whatever ecstasy you have experienced, let compassion and forgiveness become your companions. Feel their beloved virtues in each hand, walking you home when you are lost, blazing a trail forward as new adventures call. A wild and rugged frequency inhabits the primal cycles of life and death, of rest and activation, of light and darkness.

Become a dancer inside the sea of love. Embrace the winds of intimacy as part of your birthright and your evolution. Let this movement be initiated by an unwavering, deep self-acceptance. No longer seek approval elsewhere, build your own bliss fortress within. Be willing to shed fixed roles and part with the tired, old narratives. Say farewell to outmoded ways of living. This is true liberation.

Look for the glimmers of joy and freedom in your daily existence. Listen to the tree's sway, witness the birds sing, look up at the infinite sky. Doing this will purify your vision and bless your soul.

Love is artistry in motion, beauty in movement—an ever soft, timeless embrace. Love is the inward journey towards healing ourselves and the world. Love is an electric, alchemical frequency that ushers all life—plant, animal, human—into form. Love is the baseline by which we evolve, create, and beautify the world. Love is the mysterious, primal, and generative source of all creation.

To love yourself wholly is the radical yet delicate balancing act between being boundless and devotional, sovereign and committed.

The spark of rebirth lives inside each moment. The magnetic force of your authentic love will reveal the lurking shadows and brighten the faithful path before you. Every soul, space, and home you grace will receive your light. Each heart you touch becomes more whole, kind, and wise.

No longer hide your wild heart. Let it be known; share it vast and free. Make a vow to your highest self to embody the fullest love you can every day. You are invited to heal and called to be in loving service to life. Watch the tender and evolutionary effects of your love ripple out into the world.

Practices for Embodying the Lover

~

The Lover's Recalibration: A Visualization and Breath Practice

Intention

To clear imbalance and infuse the body with the power of love.

Set your intention to soften and open to the power of love.

Light a candle. Find a comfortable seat. You will be working with the colors of the rainbow to recalibrate the body. (Read through once, and then try with your eyes closed.)

Begin by connecting to your breath for two minutes—long full exhales to release tension, slow and steady inhales to welcome compassion and love.

Imagine a healing white light in the form of a ring several inches over your head.

This ring holds the seven colors of the rainbow: red, orange, yellow, green, blue, indigo, and violet.

Visualize each color being pulled down to a specific area in the body, take six deep breaths, infusing your body with a sense of compassion or self-love.

Red: Locate this color in the ring and pull it down your crown and your spine. Let it land at your tailbone, pubic bone, sitting bones, and from there down into the earth. Welcome your grounded, loving self.

Orange: Locate this color, pull it down through your crown and spine and let it infuse your pelvis. Soften to receive your creative, sensual, embodied Lover within.

Yellow: Locate this color, pull it down your crown and spine, and let it ignite your solar plexus. Let each breath ignite your internal spark of love and welcome your inner power.

Green: Locate this color, pull it down through the crown and spine. Let it swirl in your heart, lungs, arms, and hands. Allow any guarding around your heart to soften. Merge with the power of love as the source all of creation. Let it become fully embodied.

Blue: Locate this color, pull it down through the crown, and let it embrace your throat and the back of your neck. Breathe into the freedom to speak your truth. Open your ears to listen to the sound of love within. Inhale to love, exhale to love.

Indigo: Locate this color, pull it down into the crown, and let it swirl inside your mind to clear all thoughts away. Connect to the frequency of love. Let this color pour out of the forehead and the back of the head. Welcome your intuitive gifts.

Violet: Locate this color, pull it down into the crown, and let it become a fluid channel into your whole body. Visualize a cocoon of light enveloping you. Allow your breath to become love. Your whole body and mind are now merging with the essence of love.

Return to your breath and feel the earth below you. Seal in sacred space, thanking yourself for this recalibration.

Observe any sensations. Journal any messages, symbols or feelings received.

Note: These colors may shift as you practice this technique. You may also feel sensations in your body, you may experience energetic and emotional releases, and you may receive symbols, sounds or images. Stay open to this process.

A Lover's Blessing
Today I say yes to love.
I choose to infuse my heart, body and mind with goodness.
I lay down the perceptions that diminish my compassion.
I slide out of the narratives that block me from loving myself
and others fully. I allow my spirit to be steeped in loving
awareness long enough to cleanse the residue of loss,
pain, and unhappiness.

Breath by breath, I forgive and begin again.
I return to the temple of love.
You, my friend, my lover, I hold you
in your spiraled depths, in your tragic moments of despair,
in your ecstatic, synchronistic flow.
I will be your witness. I will be your Lover.
Your best friend. I will give you the space needed
while walking this path of life with you.

All the while I promise to blaze a trail in my own soul's quest.
In adoration of this crazy duality of love, I will see you for who
you are, not for who you are not. A promise from my lips, a
tender kiss from the cavern of my soul.
I will meet you in the temple of love.

Seven Days of Love Liberation: A Compassionate Cleanse

Intention
Track the drama in body, mind, and actions; with compassion.

Make a commitment to yourself to practice compassion for seven days. Begin each morning by lighting a candle, sitting in silence for two to five minutes, and welcoming a warm, soft love within.

Follow this with two to five minutes of free-flow journal practice on the theme of living with compassion. Journal the ways you are not kind to yourself. Be completely honest and write all the unkind things you say in your mind about self and others.

Then set a vision for your day by calling in three or more gratitudes, along with three calls to actions to invite loving kindness. Be very clear: for example, "I commit to being in nature today; I commit to eating healthy food; I commit to being off screen and having a candlelight bath before bed."

For the seven days, begin and end your days with a morning ritual and an evening ritual.

Observe when you are not being compassionate, document it in your journal. This is a very effective practice. Over time, you will set the lower, habitual thoughts free and more readily choose to return to self-love.

Practice the art of forgiveness when you fall off track, let it all go, and repeat this affirmation: "I am a vessel of compassion, I am love, I am peace, I am here."

Seal in your final day of practices by celebrating your devotion to the path of compassion. Take yourself on a self-care date—see an art show, spend a day in nature, or engage in something that expands love within.

Awaken the Sensual Goddess: The Lover's Dance

Intention

To clear the blockages of pain, grief, and tension, and to ignite your sensual self-love and your wild heart.

Find music that inspires you to move.

Set your timer for five to ten minutes.

Light a candle and set an intention to clear anything but radical self-love and freedom in body and mind.

Warm up your body by rolling your shoulders, circling your hips, shaking, and tapping any body parts that feel numb or blocked.

With your hands, vigorously tap your upper chest. Relax your jaw and allow the sound of "aah . . ." to stream out of you.

When it feels right begin to move, dance, sway, jog on the spot—anything that gets your body moving. This is a dance for you to express your inner wild woman. Hold nothing back, get lost in the dance. Sometimes we need to move fast, sweat, and sing, or allow toning or moaning sounds to come out. Let it be a shamanic journey in the form of movement. Be in awe of your ability to self-guide and rebalance your love channels.

When you feel complete, lie down, relax completely, and observe any messages or sensations in the body. A symbol, an insight, or an affirmation may come to you.

Journal about your experience.

Soul Care Practices to Embody the Lover

Dress in clothes that give you a sensual, creative, and empowered feeling.

Write poetry, love letters to self and others.

Practice meditation, focusing on amplifying the frequency of love and self-acceptance.

Receive supportive healing practices from professionals to clear childhood wounds.

Practice one form of self-love daily and record it.

Nourish yourself with enough water and healthy food daily.

Create time to be in nature and to restore your energy every day.

Observe where you give your love power away. Change tracks.

Take a candlelit ritual bath with essential oils and rose petals, consciously welcoming self-love.

Journal Prompts for Integrating the Lover Within

The Embodied Lover's Characteristics
Sensual | Emotionally Mature | Sovereign | Unafraid of Intimacy
Forgiving | Self-Aware | Fluid | Vulnerable

Ask yourself these questions to infuse more consciousness and intimacy into your personal love journey.

What does the flow of loving energy feel like in my body?

What restricts the flow of love? What are the conditions or the triggers?

How can you become more aware the moment you turn away from love, and redirect yourself?

Create a "I am _____" or "I will _____" statement that will remind you of the power of love when you get lost in disconnection, fear, or anger.

What do you love about yourself today? Name three things. Do this naming practice as you do your daily gratitudes.

What daily practices or actions return you to the state of self-love and compassion?

How can you express your pure, unconditional love to others today? Giving love generates love.

Journal Prompts to Work with the Lover's Shadow

Shadow Characteristics of the Lover
Dramatic | Afraid of Intimacy | Obsessed with Image
Defended | Unaware | Self-Critical
Disconnected from Body | Uncompassionate

What habitual patterns do you see inside your current relationship to yourself, and others?

What interrupts your ability to forgive or let go of the smaller, daily interruptions or triggers in life? And how can you attempt to return to the power of love with more ease and grace next time?

What brings you to feel grief, despair, or sadness?

Free-write a list of what offers nourishment to your heart, body, and mind when in this state.

How and why do you avoid vulnerability?

Do you fear intimacy? Can you track where this comes from? Is there something that is ready to be revealed or a commitment to self-love ready to be named? Free-write about this.

Pink Crush

Pink crush, hush—the early dawn stirs my soul awake.
Crescent moon like a crown upon the mountain fortress.
I move in and decide to stay a while.

Hope of a new beginning, a soft, snowy blanket of virgin terrain.
Each step bearing faith. Love exists inside sorrow.
Ever sweet, the chickadee's song touches
upon the vulnerability of all existence.

A brave one, to be so small in this vast universe of wild happenings.
The paradoxical edges of this life become palpable—
lightness to dark, truth to untruth, suffering to ecstasy.
Like lovers entangled in a field of dreams, endlessly holding on.

As the sun's majesty rises over the dappled conifers,
Time stands exquisitely still.
To carry this infinite torch is to love with reckless abandon.
(Suddenly, I witness the bitterness in my mouth
transform into sweetness.)
I dwell here—with curiosity inside this perfect pause.
Lost inside the dance of love.

The Mystic

". . . there was a new voice
which you slowly
recognized as your own,
that kept you company
as you strode deeper and deeper
into the world . . ."

Mary Oliver

Chapter 6

Awakening the Mystic
Truth Seeker, Vision Holder, Divine Space Explorer

Transcending time, magnifying space, echoes of sublime chants,
cryptic yet familiar—an invitation.
Old soul, star gazer, ceremonialist, light carrier,
dream creatress, weaver of the numinous.
The Mystic stirs, churns, and morphs into unbounded presence.
A palpable, enigmatic frequency streams
galaxies of source knowledge—
she speaks truth for the good of all.
Guided by intuitive presence,
her rhythmic ecosphere overcomes self-prescribed illusions.

No longer ignoring the whispers, dreams, visions,
rather she becomes a conduit for timely foresights.
As the ethereal planes comes alive, she is quiet, deeply listening.
Cricket song, moon glow, monarch wing, fossils lost and found.
Flashes of past happenings suddenly make sense.
Each memory building her spirit house alive.
Salt of the earth, an aura cocooned by a golden, fine silk weave.
Blurring and bridging, the ordinary and mysterious merge into one.
A crafted frequency of faith in the ephemeral, otherworldly presence.
The temple doors swing open into a living sanctuary
of her alchemical intelligence.
The world awakens.

Who Is the Mystic?

Anchored to the earth and attuned to her inner voice, the feminine Mystic embodies an otherworldly, enigmatic presence. Drawn to the numinous, spirited, and ethereal frequencies, she imbibes natural magic and shares it freely with the world.

The Mystic holds a unique capacity to harmonize her emotional states while also having a well-developed intuition. She actively develops her listening powers. Aware of supernatural happenings, the Mystic can see beyond the drama and stressors of daily life. This allows her to stay connected to the wondrous, wild realm of source and mystery.

The modern Mystic trusts the power of divine timing. She embodies a heightened awareness to what happens in the natural world and to the ordinary synchronicities in everyday life. Compelled to follow those signs and signals, the Mystic moves through life's whirlwind of joys and challenges with a grounded yet vast perspective.

The Mystic understands that the deepest calling is attuning to the authentic voice within. The impulses derived from her own knowing expand consciousness in all the dimensions—physical, mental, emotional, and spiritual. Attention to her inner voice, when she is anchored in the present moment and free of past limitations, is the portal into the Mystic's spiritual matrix.

The Mystic walks the earth sharing her gifts with all sentient beings while tuning in to the realm of the skies. She is a holder of ethereal wisdom. Her nature is of mud and star; she is both dark and light. She carries the fluid essence of life-giving water and the transformative forces of the sun and moon. She is salt of the earth, grounded and raw, intermixed with glimmers of ancient star wisdom. There is a magic, and a clarity that is unforgettable in the Mystic's nature.

The feminine Mystic is the beloved holder of many lineages, matriarchs, and dimensions. She is able to have deep, meaningful, and intimate relations with those on earth. Judgement does not cloud her vision or separate her from others. It's as if she is a walking vessel of compassionate, worldly wisdom.

Mystics are the bridges between other realms, worlds, cultures, and people. Practices to enhance the inner life include visualization, meditation, voice work, soul care rituals, body–mind alignment, and artistic pursuits. Over time this work fosters communication channels with the higher self, which leads to a felt sense of the unspoken and unseen realms. Intuitive and psychic gifts begin to come alive. These deeper experiences transform the Mystic into guide, healer, thought leader, manifester, and visionary. The developed Mystic holds a container of wisdom that allows her to be calm in the state of crisis and problem solving while not taking on excess stress, pain, or grief. The natural Mystic can form deep friendships yet is just as comfortable in the company of herself and the natural world.

The Mystic sees from the eyes of her soul and lives an empowered, meaningful existence. The Mystic is both receptive to her inner landscape and aware of energy in her external ecosystem. Naturally, she can bridge worlds between the mundane and the extraordinary. Inside this frequency, the ephemeral, breathtaking, simple, and deeply moving moments return her to love, faith, and wonder in the world.

Why Align with Your Inner Mystic?

The undiscovered Mystic does not believe in the power of listening to intuitive whispers. She forces her willpower on others to get what she wants. She is not connected to her feelings, nor does she understand how her negativity or judgement affects others. The Mystic lost in the shadow is unable to discern truth from illusion; she may present herself outwardly as something she is not. The undeveloped Mystic cannot visualize her intentions, life goals, and dreams. Therefore, she creates a fractured life path ruled by illusion and drama, leaving her feeling unfulfilled. Essentially, the Mystic living in the shadows exhausts her inner vision, experiences fragmentation and confusion about her true nature, and ends up disconnected from life's deeper calling.

If you have lost sight of your dreams, developing your inner Mystic will radically shift the way you direct your life. If you are at a crossroads in your life, awakening the inner Mystic will give you a new perspective. Inviting the Mystic to ignite the sacred within will reveal limiting habits and thought patterns that keep you from living your deepest purpose. When you direct your attention inwards daily, through quiet contemplative moments, you build your capacity to listen to the pure essence within.

The feminine Mystic's power is expansive. Energy can be sensed within, above, below, and all around. She uses this information to respond to her soul's calling. Paying close attention to the sacred experiences coming alive in this human body is the work of the Mystic. Receiving powerful support and affirmations from the universe to keep living the life that she is most passionate about is the gift. Enabling the messages, signs, symbols, muses, and guides to inform the present-moment inquiries and the next steps is her craft. Through believing, feeding, and devoting oneself to the inner work, magic and divine timing will arrive in the most auspicious places.

The task is to stay awake.

To tap into the superpowers of the Mystic is to transform life situations for the greater good of self and humanity. You will feel as if the light has turned on and you are seeing from a whole new perspective. No longer do you feel the universe conspiring against you, rather you understand your place in this world—your presence is essential. You will be able to speak your truth unapologetically and trust that your unique gifts are to be shared with the world.

Having genuine faith in the unfolding of life's daily mysteries generates space for divine timings, unexplainable synchronicities, and "aha" moments. Give your inner Mystic permission to come alive. Be the life gate into the world of the sacred. The treasures of wonder, joy, and deep peace are right here inside you. When sourced and shared freely, every ounce of this precious earthside existence becomes the magnetic weave of your soul's true calling.

Visualization and Language: A Gateway into the Mystic's Manifestation Process

The powers of the imaginal realm, when awakened, can truly transform your life. When you can *see* something, it becomes more likely that you can access its energetic process and speak clearly about it. If you want to shift certain things about your life, yet you cannot access the power of your imagination to visualize the result you want, or use empowered language to get it, it is far less likely to happen. If you don't believe in your power to make the change, this creates a fracture in your energy field. You essentially give away mystical insight. You must *see* and *believe* something for it to be embodied and created. Using clear, positive language in tandem with visualization is an essential step towards embodied manifestation.

Visualization needs time and space to be practiced, in daily moments of contemplation. At first, you may need guidance from teachers to learn meditative skills and tools. Over time, the work of the Mystic is to self-guide into different states of consciousness. Focusing on the inward journey becomes a personal and sacred practice.

Start in your morning meditation by visualizing the events of your day unfolding the way you would like to see them. At first, it will be normal to hear your mind race, witnessing random thoughts and bantering negative self-talk. A visualization practice can support you in cleaning up your inner dialogue. The inner work of the Mystic is to sort through energy and experience as it arises, to acknowledge and detach from negative thinking. Over time, the practice becomes simply observing the thoughts and releasing any attachment or association with them.

Through this training, you become less attached to the narrative of the wounded inner child or pain from the past. When it arises, you can look the pain in the eyes and embrace who you are now—today—not who you were in the past. Paying attention to inner dialogue, the way you listen and speak to yourself is the Mystic's craft. She chooses not to lose her energy through unnecessary drama.

Her ability to visualize and direct her current ship through the vast sea of possibility keeps her steady. She engages with the unseen and ethereal realms while remaining anchored in the here and now.

The practice of visualization supports the journey within to feel what attachments and lower frequencies we may be feeding. The art of untangling them to see what then wants to grow is how the Mystic feeds the essential self. Through this perspective and lifestyle shift, connecting to one's core intention and visualizing it already in the manifest generates a deeper source of life energy. The work then becomes gathering the pieces to enliven the vision. Choose your words wisely; generate them to align with a positive frequency. Be it a major life change or a simple shift in being, if one cannot visualize and speak to the transformation, it will seem arduous, out of reach, and ultimately unattainable.

With devotion and trust, the gateway into the evolving self opens. Intuitive glimmers, divine guidance, and symbols or clues are received. The Mystic prayerfully gathers the pieces, weaving them together with great attention. All the while building her soul house, creating the life she already knows—for she has seen it before.

Bridging Worlds:
From the Ordinary to the Mysterious

Embracing the mysterious and untamed energies in life brings us closer to the divine pulse of life itself. The call of the Mystic attuned to the divine feminine frequency is to observe, refine and name the day-to-day events within the ordinary and the sacred so that we may birth our visions alive with support and freedom. To engage in "who we are" or "how we live" in relationship to the mundane and extraordinary existence in daily life greatly contributes to an expanded awareness of personal, collective, and planetary energy. Understanding that we too can bridge the worlds between the physical and the spiritual opens the realm of the imaginal. Accepting both the factual and the unexplainable allows our intuitive capacities to evolve. Somehow, we loosen our grip on controlling the outcome of every situation. We live more spontaneously. We embody a state of flow that allows the egoic mind to rise above the inner critic and to dream into the unimaginable. This perception becomes a living frequency that generates a deeper sense of belonging on the earth, and more meaningful connections in service, purpose, and community. We become courageous in our vision and devoted to sharing our gifts with the world.

Over time the embodied mind–body bridge expands into compassionate living, into courageous loving, and magnetic fields of possibility. What once seemed unattainable transforms into the seeable and the doable. Trusting in the mysterious paradigm of divine timing and right action generates space to sense, see, hear, and feel subtle energy. We more readily follow the intuitive calls and feel the close support of another presence—spiritual or physical.

Living in harmony with the earth and moon cycles will naturally allow us to enter these states, facilitated by the primal, elemental channels of earth, air, fire, water, and ether.

When we are no longer ruled by hard facts, we open to the wonder and magic that surrounds us. As we bridge the worlds, we expand this luminous yet simple intelligence. We begin to express courage, goodness, and trust that inspire others to follow their dreams. To pay it forward and be the wisdom carriers innately born through the legacy of life forms in the past, present and those coming, encourages us to keep doing the work.

It takes discipline and courage to pursue and trust in the mysterious. Make peace with the confusion, struggle, and lack of clarity, just as you are at peace with the known, explainable, and concrete realities in your life. Ride the waves of internal inquiry as much as you do your external experience. Become a witness to both and take space to ensure you remain true to your own path. It's so easy to get lost in an endless sea of distraction, following others, and hiding out in fear or inertia. We are always navigating the inner compass of life. Each day is a blessing and an opportunity to begin again. There is always new terrain to explore, and another life passage to enter. The crossroads in life require compassionate presence and accountability; you must be willing to see what is ready to evolve, re-invent, or re-structure itself from within your core. The flame of presence and inquiry into your current life's calling must stay steady to generate expansion and abundance both in the ordinary and the otherworldly planes.

The Unavailable Mystic: When Illusion Rules

When attachments to external desires overpower our day to day experiences the Mystic's insight becomes inaccessible. Our mind and body can easily become polluted with toxic energy. We begin to form veils, layers or shields of illusion that shape our living reality. We forget to tend to our soul care practices. The tools we work with to birth our dreams alive are no longer working. We may turn away from what matters most to us because we have lost our way. Even if we truly long for something in life, we may feel like we don't know where to begin. When our sense of purpose becomes muddled and unclear, we most likely have lost a connection to the magical, mysterious, and wondrous aspects of life.

What we pay attention to shapes us. Perhaps we know or feel that what we are doing is not really what we want in life. Or maybe the narrative of illusion has become so deeply entrenched in the unconscious that we are disassociated from our truth. We fall into a trance and end up feeding the exact systems that we want to be free from—patriarchy, consumerism, following the norm to attempt to fit in, holding our voice back in fear of being wrong, not listening to our gut in fear of failure. At its core we fear what light us up because we have gotten so far away from it. It's uncomfortable to return to our own source. We become unhappy, unfulfilled, and disconnected from our true power. Our inner critic becomes so loud that our relationship to self and others becomes toxic. Fraught with self-judgement, we harden and shut down. We question and hide our vulnerability to cover up our own unresolved pain. We become perpetrators of our victimhood or martyrdom and lose our intuitive awareness.

The Tipping Point

When you are merely coping with life you lose sight of your intuitive intelligence. When you are just barely managing the workload of constant productivity, you feed the cycle of disconnection. The cluttered mind begins to spin and send you into altered states. Your ability to discern truth from illusion gets lost. When you can no longer access the resting places or the joyous spaces within the chaos of life, this is your tipping point.

Your inner Mystic is calling you. She urges you to interrupt the trance and surrender into silence and stillness. Ask yourself, "How do I create time and space for a balanced, wondrous, and intuitive life?" This becomes a direct call to action to tend to a deeper level of soul care.

When you long for rest and a more adventure-wonder-love-filled life, this is the universe encouraging you to return to your inner Mystic's journey. When an intuitive message or a dream suddenly stops you in your tracks, and glimmers of light pull you out of your trance, pause and listen. Surrender to the experience. This process is golden.

Spiritual Bypassing: The Misuse of Power in Spiritual Practices

Within some spiritual movements, the devotional practices, teachers, and communities can become so powerful that we lose sight of our own authenticity. As you open yourself fully to a specific faith, there is the potential to give your power away in the name of people-pleasing. Throwing yourself at the feet of the guru generates a convoluted mind–body experience. Turning away from your own core beliefs may cause you to misappropriate sacred practices and lineages and to follow blindly. This not only diminishes your sense of integrity but masks your true path towards spiritual integration. The shadowed Mystic falls into the veils of spiritual bypassing as she is not able to see through the misuse of power. This phenomenon is common in many lineages and communities in our world today.

Avoiding spiritual bypassing takes maturity, honesty, and clear thinking.

In our times, there is a tendency to romanticize spirituality and mindfulness practices. When the practices are not taught or received in an embodied way, we can become ungrounded and float halfway between the earth and the sky. At first this can seem like relief from inner pain or past trauma. Yet it may be part of a cycle of disassociation. This desire to disconnect from the events in everyday life takes us further into illusion and distances us from the source of intuitive deepening. When we turn away from our own healing work to follow a lineage, the ego may form belief systems that bolster personal and collective suffering.

Certain organized lineages of mind–body practices and world religions have been found to be fraught with hierarchical systems. People can give their power over to teachers or gurus and lose their own authentic voice. There is a very fine line between devoting oneself to an organized system and remaining sovereign. The human mind loves to follow systems and codes; these can create boundaries that make us feel safe. While it is important to have inspiring teachings and devoted practices, the systems of belief must become embodied, grounded, and clear of any form of manipulation.

Beyond Smoke and Mirrors: Grounding Is Key to Developing Your Inner Mystic

Go beyond the smoke and mirrors of certain spiritual practices. Be aware when you are following a spiritual teacher to fit into a mould or generate a false sense of security.

Ask yourself: Does this practice or path light me up or take me out of my power? Am I half-heartedly living or am I embracing this moment to its fullest? Am I feeding my own illusions and projections or does this practice give me the life force necessary to purse what matters most to me right now?

These are essential questions to hold as you enter any spiritual practice. Be mindful of your energy and where you choose to place it. With a solid, energetically clean teacher you will never feel like they are taking something away from you—stealing, distorting, or manipulating your own energy. Rather, the student–teacher relationship should be nourishing, liberating, and grounding. That self-inquiry becomes the greatest discipline of all. Having this embodied intelligence upon entering any spiritual discipline will support you in perceiving systems of hierarchy. You will maintain crystal-clear boundaries so your own energy body remains pure. This is the modern Mystic's way of exploring the spiritual arts. It's experiential, self-aware, and—what is essential—deeply grounded.

There is a natural evolution that occurs as our personal beliefs and spiritual practices shift, change, and expand throughout our life. Connecting to the inner Mystic allows you to go beyond ego driven or disjointed faith practices. Discerning what is true and what is illusion becomes the weave inside the Mystic's loom. It's a mysterious journey, and a deeply intimate, reverent process. You can get to the heart of what lights you up when you commit to listening to your inner impulses. As you experience spiritual practices and teachings, you learn to feel into how they resonate with your own values, how they support this current cycle of life, and how they inspire you to be your authentic self.

Now is the time to see beyond yourself as the center of the picture.
Let go of your inner critic. Understand the toxic residue from the
past so you may live soulfully and love deeply.
No longer play fool to the illusion of veils and surface talk.
Go deep into the abyss where the etheric energy swirls radiant
circles around your spirit.
Call to the ancient ones and ask for guidance.
Make prayers in their honor.

When you lose faith, no longer fear falling off the path;
remember that the Mystic way lies deep inside the earth
and glimmers in the starry night sky.
It arrives with the swift, fierce, and gracious winds
that shake you from your slumbered trance and
guide you home to your true nature.
There you discover your capacity to collaborate with the divine.

Mystical Muse: Hildegard of Bingen

Hildegard of Bingen was a powerful Mystic who used the power of her visions, voice, intellect, and devotional practices to share her gifts of science, spirit, and feminine leadership.

Hildegard was a Mystic, nun, composer, healer, and visionary who lived in Germany during the Middle Ages. She devoted her life to God, the spiritual arts and sharing her faith and gifts with humanity. Although she lived in a limiting patriarchy where women were not regarded as spiritual leaders, Hildegard did not let this deter her. She was a force of nature who left behind a potent collection of scholarly writings, theological manuscripts, and musical compositions.

It was not until the 1980s that her sublime songs and soul-stirring compositions were recovered and performed, allowing her artistic legacy to be known by the modern world.

In addition to Hildegard's impressive output, she was also a healer who created herbal tinctures and natural remedies to cure the ill. Throughout her monastic life, she claimed to have enlightening experiences, recorded as divine visions, astral projections, and trance-like states, where she received messages from the spiritual realms to share with her people. Religious figures would come to her for counsel. She was a woman unafraid to speak and act upon her psychic and spiritual gifts.

In her words: "I am the fiery life of the essence of God; I am the flame above the beauty in the fields; I shine in the waters; I burn in the sun, the moon, and the stars. And with the airy wind, I quicken all things vitally by an unseen, all-sustaining life."

Channel Hildegard's essence to empower your inner Mystic. Listen to Hildegard's songs and compositions to feel the exalted recollection of dwelling in the space of mystical allure.

Honor the wisdom of those who came before us, and inquire into the sacred, ethereal, and artistic planes of their visions. Sit inside the quiet devotion of your own treasure trove and feel the impulses that arise from the great mystics of the past.

Hold back no longer in life. Commit to the spirited practices that build your capacity to discern truth over illusion. Be brave and share your voice with the world. Embrace Hildegard's courageous artistry, powerful leadership, and ability to express her channeled visions as you ignite your own mystical essence. Shed the doubts of your authentic spiritual power. Like Hildegard, blaze your own path up spirit mountain; do not allow limitations, rules, or societal paradigms to hold you back from the life you desire.

Allow her sentiments to inspire you. "Glance at the sun. See the moon and the stars. Gaze at the beauty of the earth's greenings. Now, think."

Hildegard of Bingen's gifts are boundless, brave, and intelligent. Her legacy inspires the collective feminine psyche through leadership, creativity, spirituality, and science. Thus, we can access mystical mind–body states that enable our visions to come alive. With sovereignty, trust, and devotion we cast them far and wide, no longer fearing our own intuitive gifts and spiritual power.

When the Mystic Calls:
Learning How to Receive the Signals

If you find yourself too busy to create time for mind–body practices that ground and inspire you, the Mystic may be seeking your attention. If your emotions are ruling your daily existence and draining your energy, it's time to explore how the Mystic can support you.

Signs of mind–body disconnection are mind fog, lethargy, depression, lack of purpose, desensitization, overwhelm, or inability to focus. We receive signs throughout our daily life; if we are self-aware, we can get curious about what needs our attention, and possible ways to remedy the imbalances. The Mystic within you may be calling you now to remember your true calling and reconnect to your magical, intuitive, inspired self.

Your body is your living canvas. Your temple speaks, it's time to rest. Yet, your mind is a superhighway of fast thoughts, media overtakes, life hacks. Attachments are distractions. The roller coaster of emotional burnout, fatigue, lack of motivation makes you want to tune out. When you feel as if you are chasing a long-lost dream—reminiscing about the past more than you are living in the present—your inner Mystic is nudging you to cleanse yourself and begin again. What do you do? How do you respond? Now is the time for a deep dive into what is contributing to personal overwhelm.

Finding time to be in stillness is essential to the Mystic's inner matrix. Slowing down, communing with nature, grounding yourself in creative pursuits, and living in harmony with your true self are mediums to access and activate your inner Mystic. Find the places and spaces where your service and innate gifts become channeled into your purpose. This is the Mystic coming alive.

Naming What Is True in the Moment

Developing your Mystic wisdom becomes a steady, consistent journey of naming what is true and what is necessary or essential in life. In any given situation, practice asking yourself this baseline question: "Is it true and is it essential?" The walk up spirit mountain to reclaim your intuitive wisdom has begun when this question becomes your first impulse. But honoring self-truth in the moment is impossible if you are weighed down by the stressors and triggers of your past or current narrative. This work is not for the faint of heart. It takes courage, along with a daily practice, for the Mystic's voice to be expressed.

The important piece to understand here is that the inner Mystic is unavailable when you are being controlled by your external environment or failing to acknowledge what the inner environment truly needs. Social control systems keep us disconnected from our highest self; these include excess media, the modern-day productivity wound—the notion that the work is never done, and that success is defined by materialism. The desire to purchase more in order to fill an empty feeling within, to eat or drink to fill the pit of sorrow or grow numb contributes to our modern pandemic of loneliness and lack of fulfillment.

What you feed in body, mind, and spirit grows. Your body is always listening. You can choose to feed disconnection or to desensitize, or you can choose to tend to your inner rhythms first. Consciously discerning what is exhausting you and pulling you away from developing a deeper union with your inner self is the path to allowing the inner Mystic to speak. For real change to occur it must become embodied.

Carry the flame of the Mystic's sacred candle into every corner of your life. This is how the feminine brings light, love, and power to her craft. Her leadership is intuitive, clear, and all encompassing. It takes courage. And it takes work to dismantle the illusions as they arise. Let us do this work for not only ourselves, but for future generations so they may be inspired to cultivate, organize, and integrate the sacred in daily life, love, and leadership.

Feed the spirited, mystical, and meaningful frequencies within.
Loosen your grip on the rules and identities that perpetrate the
fear of not being loved, wanted, needed, held, listened to, or seen.
When in doubt go to the forest, listen to the trees.
Their wisdom is mystical, nourishing, and ancient.

Liberating the Inner Voice

Many of us lost the ability to trust our inner voice a long time ago. If you were encouraged to be a people pleaser or told to shut down your emotions, you most likely have lost touch with your ability to listen within.

To begin the liberation of your inner voice, you must track the ways in which you feed old paradigms, past narratives, or inherited family systems. Healing starts by understanding where they live, what form or expression they take, and how this affects your relationships to self and others. This is perhaps the most powerful feminine work we can do in our lifetime—to understand why we do what we do, for whom, and what we seek. Is our current belief system hard-wired from our family origin or cultural paradigms? Deep self-awareness comes from being aware of how we second guess ourselves or block our inner voice before we even have a chance to honor it. To engage in this body of work is to land back inside the simple question once again: "Is this true for me right now?" Let this very question be your guide in life.

Tuning In: A Micro Ritual to Awaken Your Inner Voice

Let us begin this discovery by taking a deep breath in and out. Consciously soften and relax into your environment. To access our inner listening, we need to let go of some preoccupations in the mind, and release tension in the body. Ask your body what it wants to express—don't censor. Ask your mind to release its fear and worries just for the next minute.

Return to your breath, maybe even close your eyes, and again ask your inner voice to speak. The work is to track the first impulse. Now locate where the listening and the voice come from. Form a compassionate relationship to what wants to be acknowledged, heard, or spoken.

Practice this daily. Your intuitive impulses will begin to guide your life.

The Living Mystic Channels

Discernment, awareness, and softening within become the channels to source the first intuitive impulse inside any situation. Sometimes it will come in the form of a symbol, color, words, or visions. The work is to receive the message, discern its origin, and either accept the impulse if it's pure to you, or release it if it's not useful or true.

Staying unattached to the outcome in this inner listening is essential, as is the ability to discern what is real and what is fabricated. Being willing to nurture your initial impulses gives peace and clarity inside the daily practices. In return, a more dimensional and expansive perspective emerges. Being attentive inside the present moment is the Mystic's superpower. If you rely solely on external forces, faiths, or teachers to dictate your own beliefs, feelings, and direction in life you will develop a dependency on external influences.

Become curious about how you ride this edge of external influences while staying connected to your inner rhythms.

The more untethered you become from the past narrative or future attachments, the more available you are to the original impulse of what wants to come forward. This is the divine feminine Mystic coming alive. We are all born with this gift, and our adult life is about reclaiming access to what matters most. Ask what brings you closer to expressing your soul essence in the world. This is how to utilize your gifts and share them freely. They become the way your spirit says, "Yes, I am here, I am listening. I am meant to do this work at this time, and this is how I balance my passions with my truth."

"Spirit and energy should be clear as the night air;
In the soundless is the ultimate pleasure all along."
Sun-Buer, Taoist Priestess, Mystic, Poet

The Mystic's Code of Ethics

Heart
Have Compassion + Be Free of Judgement + Forgive
Connect with the element of Air to purify your heart's capacity to see and feel love.

Body
Trust in Transformation + Be Your Own Healer
Welcome the power of Fire to rebalance your own energy body daily.

Emotions
Have Courage + Practice Letting Go
Be like Water, find flow and release what is not necessary to hold.

Mind
Live in Wonder + Practice Reciprocity
Look to the Earth's creations, live in awe of her bounty and beauty.

Spirit
*Cultivate Peace + Create Time for Inner Reflection +
Cast Your Prayers Out*
Open to the ethereal frequencies that dwell inside intuitive, sacred spaces and cast your prayers out into the world every day. Speak truth inside and out. Become a living vision of your embodied intuitive impulses as they generate a ripple effect of goodness in the world.

The Mystic's Matrix

Intuitive and insightful, the Mystic's energy is grounded in good faith. With a deep union with the natural world and scientific phenomena, the Mystic develops a kindred connection to the element of surprise, wonder, and life's cosmic happenings. A magical, wonder-fueled frequency bears the fruits of optimism and possibility. The

Mystic can sense the vibrations of goodness, truth, and the sacred. She aims to live her life by these codes. Inspired by the energies found in the natural world, the Mystic has a compelling magic about her gaze that inspires others to embody their own light. Enigmatic and creative, she holds the capacity to transfigure dark situations into learning moments filled with light. Ancient wisdom—awakened through codes, values, right action and sentiments—streams from the heart, mind, and mouth of the Mystic.

The Mystic Builds Her Spirit House

The Mystic engages in soulful practices to build her steady, yet always evolving inner spirit house. Weaving ways to initiate contemplative, internal practices, and rituals through her day is her craft. To discover and listen to the current inner impulses is the loom. This becomes the Mystic's daily superpower. The practice of discerning an authentic impulse versus a fear-based pattern is ongoing work. To understand how the narrative of the past limits, clouds, and feeds an illusioned life is essential. To be curious and non-attached to the outcome of an idea or vision is one of the greatest tools with which the Mystic builds her inner sanctuary. Through such devotion and dedication to self-inquiry, a deeper field of consciousness and high vibrational frequency grows. This magnetic energy inspires others to do the same. To show up as the best version of self is to consistently return to the Mystic's code of presence and truth, which naturally enlivens the essence of wonder in every step on the journey.

To ignite the inner Mystic is to take a vow to care for your highest self. It is to live with the awareness that each day is the living ceremony that guides the essential self. It is to live in faith that the present moment is the only moment. Yes, the past informs the present, and we hold our prayers and intentions to create our future.

Essential to the Mystic's wholeness is to seek balance in how we listen to the inner self, and how we attune to the external ecosystems in both the mundane and sacred realms. On the one hand track your thought patterns, use of words and language both internally and externally, and how you anchor into daily life. On the other hand, pay attention to how you connect with the otherworldly energies—dreams, visions, intuitive downloads. These two worlds must not be separated in order for wholeness inside the Mystic's vision to be received.

Are you the same person on the yoga mat or the meditation cushion as when you need to stand in your truth and affirm personal boundaries? Can you hold the Mystic's perspective while in a heated argument with a family member or while you are cooking dinner for your hungry children?

This is often a challenge in the moment; we tend to turn away from the uneasy feelings. Yet the discipline is to turn towards them. Bring a beginner's mind to the situation and be present to both your bodily sensations and to the desire to check out. This process takes patience and the willingness to let go and be vulnerable. However, the more you do it, the easier it becomes. The next breath is always waiting to bring you back home to your body.

Staying Current with Your Evolving Self

Slowing down, developing a daily meditation practice, bookending your day with a morning and evening ritual, basking in nature's rhythms, and creating times of silence will support the inner Mystic's alchemy. With a steady, rhythmic devotion to the work—and fewer media distractions—the intuitive voice will come forward. Your daily commitment is to track and trust the inner voice as it comes.

Initiate the slower, mindful practices without aiming for individual gain or enlightenment; rather engage in them in order to experience union with self and the external ecosphere. This generates an awakening of love over disconnection, of truth over fear.

Immersing yourself in nature builds your sixth sense and attunes your awareness to the greater powers. The rhythms and pure energy of the natural world teach you to trust your own way of perceiving, receiving, and understanding your inner Mystic.

Ether is the most mysterious, unexplainable of elements, and yet it is the energy that holds earth, air, fire, and water together. Its tenuous and invisible quality is associated with the celestial realms and the upper world of space. When you attune your awareness to both the seen and the unseen worlds, you begin to observe energy as it moves and shifts in each moment. Refining our ability to receive and perceive what dwells in our natural environment, we naturally begin to sense the vibrational frequency known as the ethereal plane. We pick up clues through our subtle body. We expand our vision to include wonder and magic.

Silence is a gateway to the creative impulses. The frequency of flow, grace, and conscious communication becomes a living, breathing creative process. Creativity is an inner process and journey.

Over time, the grand "who am I?" question emerges. In this precise moment, your inner Mystic has arrived to ignite a deeper inquiry into your personal and collective life experience. Be curious about how you can show up daily to work with life's obstacles and remove the stressors as they arise; this is where the magic lives.

Trusting the Impulse: Refining Clarity

When seeking clarity first ask yourself, "What is my initial impulse?" Begin to pay attention to what your gut is telling you, even if it feels a bit murky or clouded at first. Practice writing it down if it helps. Get curious about the need for validation from others.

When you consistently practice this inner listening, you learn to release the attachment to the exact outcome desired. Instead, you allow the natural flow of energy to move alongside your intention. This becomes the formula for the mysterious energies to speak, whispering to your spirit at the most auspicious times. Through the mundane to the extraordinary, soften to receive. This doesn't mean you don't plan, focus, commit, or push forward with your visions. Rather, you get crystal clear on the energy inside the intention and connect to your inner wisdom to support your process. Cast your intention far into the ethereal planes and witness its evolution in the outer world.

Once she is awakened in you, the Mystic becomes a steady force of living attuned to the sacred. She brings you into a more intimate connection to your purpose; your place in the world evolves from here. The dramas of daily life affect you less. You can access calm inside any life storm. Your desire to prove yourself right becomes less important. Your tendency to live only out of reactivity lessens because your grounded, intuitive, and awakened Mystic can discern what matters most. This allows you to access the bigger perspective in the present moment. You are not listening just to respond; you truly listen and receive what the speaker—or the inner voice—is saying. And that is how the Mystic stays current with her own evolution. The judgements, clouded vison, and second guesses fall away, and the intuitive flashes arrive at precisely the moment they are needed. This is the feminine Mystic embodied—vast, spacious, strong, and receptive all at once.

The Mystic Way

To dream your life into being is to live
with a Mystic's natural sense of awe,
while honoring the highest goodness inside any situation.

The willingness to be mesmerized, awe-struck,
and moved by the simplest findings in nature becomes the way
in which the Mystic builds authenticity over illusion and false
perceptions. The divine feminine evokes the natural Mystic as the
sublime jewel inside the lotus flower. She sees inside the darkness
as much as the light. Her roots are nourished by deep muddy
waters as she climbs towards the sun.

The Mystic seeks the quiet of the new moon time, drawing into
its fertile alchemy for inner-life rejuvenation. Renewal is nectar

for her evolving soul—sometimes she needs to stay in the dark a while. As the next wave of intuitive callings arrive, she gathers her resources, builds momentum, and prepares to birth her visions alive. The magnetic pull of the full moon's radiance is palpable. The life gate opens, and with pure attention, she emerges whole. Like a spring flower, she unfurls into its impeccable glory. The steppingstones across this wild river of life—both precarious and swift flowing, emerges before her.
She accepts the invitation.

The feminine Mystic way carries the lineage of the wisdom keepers—the mother of all source and creation. Welcome your inner Mystic to be fully expressed. Let go of perfection, pray often, commit to serving your body as your temple, and purify your mind of lower frequencies. Deep down you have always known the power of your vision.

Live your truth—no longer doubt your wisdom.
It's time to listen more deeply than before. Be still inside the frequency of soundlessness to understand more about who you are. Open your eyes to see the ecosystem around you. Show up and nurture yourself radically. Enliven your matriarchal lineage with a life-reviving force and carry this legacy forward. Gather your pearls from raw stone. Weave the threads that are most meaningful to you. We are all ready for this steady, fierce, and deeply potent sacred femme era. History in the books. Leadership in the making. We are already here, sourcing our wisdom, gathering by the ceremonial fires—singing our songs of life's deepest callings to come alive.

Practices for
Embodying the Mystic

~

Guided Visualization:
Awakening the Mystical Field of Energy

Intention
To merge with a supporting frequency that
will ignite your intuition, purify your vision,
and empower mind–body clarity.

Begin to attune to your breath and soften your body completely. Imagine any stress or projections of past or future events fall away. Let any thoughts from your ordinary life simply slide away from your consciousness.

Visualize a supporting energy that is present, attuned, and compassionate. This guide may take the form of a person, animal, element, symbol, color, or an affirmation. Do not doubt your choice, go with it. With each inhale, fully embody the supporting frequency. Let each exhale fill the entire space with this positive essence. The supporting energy may shift and evolve. Pay attention to how the colors, patterns, shapes, and energies may want to transform. Simply receive them.

Now, specifically direct your attention to the center of your body. Invite your breath and the supporting frequency to merge at your center. Imagine it traveling through your inner landscape, purifying your body of any darkness, fear, or imbalance. You may sense where your inner energy feels blocked. See the blocks with compassion, allow them to soften.

Observe how your supporting guide or energy wants to move through you now—it's abundant, nourishing, and ready to embrace you on a deeper soul level. Allow your inner Mystic to speak to you and your ecosphere.

Create an affirmation or a prayer to immerse yourself completely in this frequency of support. Your affirmation may sound something like this, "I am grateful to receive your support, I am ready, open, and committed to doing the soul work required of me at this time. Come to me in my dreams, send me signs in my everyday life. I have faith that the messages will arrive in divine timing, and my grounded, inspired vessel will carry the good work forward."

Observe what arises in this kind of prayerful inquiry. Notice any feelings or sensations of either resistance or flow. Feel your breath back in the center of your body. Find your anchor to the earth, feel the space you are in, and give thanks to all energies present.

This Mystical frequency is yours to explore and personalize. You can invite this positive frequency in times of fear, stress, and chaos. Know that you can shift your perspective and dial into a higher vibration—one of non-judgement, compassion, and truth.

It may be helpful to journal about your experience.

Seal in this visualization by reading "A Mystic's Affirmation" aloud.

A Mystic's Affirmation

I give thanks for this day of deepening my connection to the source of life. I awaken my eyes to see the radiant life force all around me. I am intentional with the words I choose to speak—elevating both the listener, and my own listening body and mind. I am humble in my actions.

I understand how negativity dims my ability to see the magic and truth in my daily life. I pick myself up when I fall into the caves of illusion. I trust in the power of divine timing to navigate my ship back home. I am supported by my compassionate guides. My daily life choices are empowered by my capacity to trust in the greater good of humanity while seeing the bigger picture. I am discerning

*where to not put my energy to keep my inner temple clear.
My kindred practices of stillness, communing with nature,
and meditative moments become the channels in which I
keep my vessel clean. I hold my prayers and dreams in their
highest frequency and trust that when they are ready, their
sacred essence will come alive.*

⁓

The Mystic's Compass:
Navigating with the Lunar Cycle

Intention
*To honor the New Moon and the Full Moon
as anchor points to activate intuition.*

New Moon Symbolism and Rituals

New Moon is the beginning of the moon's cycle and can be embodied like a monthly initiation or "check-in." It is a highly intuitive time and requires softer, more contemplative, and internal engagements.

Ask yourself this simple question at New Moon: "What am I ready and willing to begin?" This could be an attitude, action, or a behavior.

A candlelit bath, cooking wholesome food, a restorative yoga practice, water color painting, reading poetry, visualizing your month ahead or creative writing are all ways to engage with the New Moon.

Full Moon Symbolism and Rituals

Full moon is a time of expansion, manifestation, and full expression. This is a time where drama, chaos, or overwhelm may take over if you are not aware of your current triggers and conditions.

Grounding practices such as breathwork, nature time, free movement, crystal cleansing, moon gazing, and gathering in like-minded community allows us to tune into our own bodies, clear our minds, and become inspired by what we love.

This simple question, "what can I release?," will keep you spacious in your intuitive process. The work is to take one small step and activate something nourishing and generative for yourself.

~

A Mystic's Recalibration Ritual

Intention
To clear overwhelm and awaken
an intuitive mind–body frequency.

Light a candle. Take a deep breath and relax your body while gazing at the flame of the candle.

Visualize the light of the candle coming into the center of your body. Place one hand on heart, and one hand on your center.

Attune your attitude to trust that you are in exactly the right place you need to be in your life to receive synchronicity, flow, and divine timing.

Close your eyes, draw your awareness inwards, and imagine your body as an intuitive channel.

Name three current fears or stressors and visualize them leaving your body.

Call forward three or more gratitudes and infuse your body and the space you are in with a warm, luminous vibration.

Visualize the events of your day or life and see them the way you want them to flow.

Call forward higher levels of support: "I am ready and willing to receive support at this time in my life. I am in the flow; I am a bridge between the known and the unknown aspects of my life." Write this statement down, and allow it to become your attitude, frequency, vibration.

Reveal the Energy Drain: A Bridging Exercise

Intention

To reveal the negative self-talk and actions that are stealing your energy and blocking your intuitive, mystical power.

Set your timer for nine minutes.

Do not censor any words, let the words flow freely.

Write out your top three core values—what matters most to you, codes you aim to live by. For example: self-love, creativity, honoring the spiritual path.

Take each core value and write about the ways in which you may be blocking its power with unclear energy. Are your inner thoughts negative? Are your actions feeding drama, fear, or victimization?

Create an affirmation that honors your core values through positive alignment and action in your daily life. For example: *I am a fluid channel of creativity, self-love, and spiritual honoring. I release the self-talk and actions that muddle my mystical frequency. I invite each day as a creative, loving, and spirited experience.*

Journal Prompts to Empower the Mystic

The Embodied Mystic's Characteristics
*Worldly | Spiritual, Vast | Grounded | Weaver of the Numinous
Clear | Magical | Conscious*

What practices or conditions bring you closer to your own inner impulses? What practices allow you to feel connected and conscious in your life?

What practices support you in speaking your truth?

How do you connect or commune with supporting, mystical energies daily? Is it through the elements or the natural world you find this connection? Or is it through developing an inward listening or meditation practice?

What practices or experiences bring you closer to the ethereal, mystical, or unseen realms?

Where do you source wonder, joy, and creativity in your life?

In what ways can you commit to enhancing these energies and aligning with their frequency daily?

My creative outlets are _____

My intuition is most powerful when _____

My current supporting visions are _____

I have faith in _____

I believe in _____

I trust _____

I can sense magic in _____

My inner Mystic comes alive when _____

Journal Prompts to Work with the Mystic's Shadow

Shadow Characteristics of the Mystic

Lost, Fragmented | Exhausted | Confused | Disconnected
Living in Illusion | Non-Believer | Negative

Imagine your body as a storyteller. Let it speak to your inner self-talk that is negative or diminishes your power: How can you clean up the limiting words you speak about self and others?

Name the ways you don't trust your instincts or turn away from listening to your inner impulses.

How do you feed toxic frequencies of stress, fear, or illusion in your self-talk? Are there any triggers or conditions that contribute to this situation?

How do you create space for quiet, stillness, and inner listening?

How can your inner awareness and your intuitive voice speak to generate a positive perception and enhance the quality of your life?

The Winged Perceiver

Trust in your artistry, service your craft,
answer the call to be your own guide.
Release the need to have every step and detail in place.
Get big with your vision—believe in the power of deep listening.
Your devotion to show up to your daily practice
is faith in the making.
Faith in nature and compassionate living
is your church, synagogue, mosque, temple.

Your body becomes your living altar.
Your mind, the fields to garden.
Your soul a living, breathing, and awake stream of receptivity.

Feel the winged perceiver in you come alive—precariously stand-
ing still at the cliff's edge. The rugged shoreline stones weathered
over centuries, the crashing waves speak history—
the rhythmic force of the tides drawing in, rolling out.
The constellations, the moon's shifting glow, the epic sun, and
rains, all bearing witness to this mystical symphony.

Surrender into the uncharted waters.
Take your whole self—every lesson learned, pain endured, dance
party made, untruth told, the humbling to the core.
Bring it all as you leap, arms spread, wings unfurled,
heart expanded, mind spacious.

Dive into the freedom to be the wild Mystic that you are.

The Queen

"Each one of us matters, has a role to play, and makes a difference. Each one of us must take responsibility for our own lives, and above all, show respect and love for living things around us, especially each other."

Jane Goodall

Chapter 7

The Queen

Knowledge Weaver, Vision Activator, Evolved Leader

It hit me like a surge of lightning.
A lifetime of task-mastering into dizzy exhaustion.
Scurrying into a spell of useless perfectionism.
Attempting to be the Queen of due diligence,
the martyr of the universe.
Body tightens. Breath constricts.

Distortion fueled by self-abandoned,
colonial rules of words upon worlds.
Exhausting myself to be sure
I don't feel what I am not wanting to feel.
The interior impulses call louder than ever—
the inner Queens stirs.

Stopped in my tracks; the luminaries reveal long forgotten codes.
Feet rooted in squishy mud; the spring rains are relentless.
So are the tears.
Aging is a revolutionary journey.
I hear more. See more. Feel more.
And in that moment, my lens widens.
A soul truth made into a vow; I bow to listen.
To no longer feed the noise around me.
But to welcome the messenger home.

Mind channels cleansed. Vision refined.
Cast it all unabashedly to the stars.
The constellations will hold my prayers.
The invitation becomes the initiation.
Standing at the forefront of my life,
I dwell inside the sanctuary of my expanding soul.

Who Is the Queen?

The Queen is a deeply initiated, powerful visionary who weaves her knowledge across the world to be in service to her soul's calling. She is a wise woman who crafts, strategizes, and organizes her passions and shares them unapologetically with the world. The Queen makes courageous decisions for the betterment of humanity.

The Queen embodies wholeness. She is a clear channel of refined inner strength. She is both movement and stillness, wisdom and inquiry, surrender and activation. The Queen has come to peace with the unknown and does not waste her vitality on excessive worrying. Nor does she try to make sense of things that are not worthy of her time. She has learned to let go, digest the lessons learned, and move on effectively and efficiently to be in service of her vision.

Crafting a personal sanctuary is part of the Queen's sacred constellation. Honoring divine timing through clearing her thought channels and trusting her gut instincts is part of her matrix. She doesn't wait for everything to be perfectly lined up before she acts; she utilizes the resources available to her in the moment and strikes when the iron is hot. She does not fall into the narrative of the "drama queen" who wields power over others, sensationalizes everything, or demands to be waited upon.

The Queen embodies an unforgettable presence that exudes a devoted passion to her chosen cause. She tends to her spirit through practices such as meditation, counseling, nature immersion, and alternative healing rituals. She knows she must stay attentive to body, mind, and heart. Her daily practice is to clear out the stress, pain, and drain of others; this keeps her spirit bright.

Speech is her craft; she uses language, articulation, and clarity to bring her visions alive. The Queen gathers her support team and loves to collaborate. She knows many hands make light work. Her thirst for continued knowledge in her field of service is infectious. She draws out the best in those who cross her path.

Her shadow lurks in her perfectionist tendencies, her overly analytical and critical mind, and her desire to control all aspects of her life. Once the shadowed Queen begins to unravel from such tendencies, she finds her true power—steeped in vitality, ingenuity, and resourcefulness. Her ability to surrender, practice true vulnerability, and live with humility becomes the portal to her impeccable powers of manifestation.

The embodied Queen has arrived through her lived experience of all the other archetypes. The archetypal steppingstones along the river of life usher the Queen into her own awakening—the Maiden's zest for wild hearted living, the Mother's tender embrace of her inner child, the Sage's intuitive powers, the Huntress's inner strength, the Lover's sensual yet revolutionary self-love, and the Mystic's spiritual awakening. It is the Queen who answers the call to embody the fullness of each archetypal design and come home into the power she has known to be hers all along.

"Character—the willingness to accept responsibility for one's own life—is the source from which self-respect springs."
Joan Didion

Embody the Queen: Evolving the Feminine Way

The modern Queen encourages us to take the seat of the soul. She urges us to devote this precious life to evolving consciousness through life-long learning, service, and leadership. When we step into our

Queenship, everyone benefits. To embody the Queen is to create positive change in self and others. Many will resist the invitation to accept the crown of their own feminine soul by getting caught up in the shadows, being the people pleaser, the perfectionist, the victim of unworthiness.

Yet great planetary shifts are taking place now. We are at the climax of transformation, environmentally and culturally. Time is of the essence. Pivoting away from old thought patterns is the new feminine way of leadership. Now is the time to embody your inner Queen.

Environmental activist Greta Thunberg says: *"You are never too small to make a difference."*

Does the Queen wait until the end of her life to make change in the world? No, she activates and attunes to where her service is most needed and effective.

The evolved Queen devotes herself to whatever she chooses: career, artistry, family, or relationship. No longer is the Queen about self-sacrifice and fulfilling other people's visions. The embodied Queen invests in taking time for herself and attuning to her own healing journey. At her core, she believes her time on earth is for the evolution of self to the highest levels of consciousness possible. Wise beyond her time, the Queen embodies the power of transforming heart, soul, and mind in service to this evolutionary impulse.

The Queen's superpowers are expansive and abundant. Her continued hunger for knowledge, honing her craft, and evolving her own beliefs keep her mind channels bright. She remains open to the changing tides, and the shifts in the way she leads herself, family, and her team.

As a quintessential thought leader—compassionate, spirited, and wise beyond present-day problems—the embodied Queen trusts in the divine order of right action. She inspires others to no longer dismiss their personal power, nor play victim or martyr in their life. With her crown aglow, the Queen's finesse for greatness, alongside her tireless service in the world, grants others permission and inspiration to do the same.

The era of the quiet, invisible, and backseat female is over. The modern Queen archetype has arrived to ignite feminine leadership and inner power in a way that is unapologetic, bold, loving, and revolutionary.

"Fight for the things that you care about but do it in a way that will lead others to join you."

Ruth Bader Ginsberg

Perfectionism Is Overrated: Activating Intention as the Path to Freedom

Freeing your mind from its attachment to perfectionism will enhance every area of your life. Working through the critical mind, observing your own fixation on needing to control and have things done your way is the Queen's work.

You may have been born with distinct idiosyncrasies or you may have adopted perfectionist tendencies because of your lived experience. The task is to observe and understand the ways in which your tendencies disrupt the quality of your life. How does this affect the people around you? Does your obsessive or distracted thinking steal time away from your creative projects, or does your fear of others judging you not allow you to pursue your dreams? Do you hold back in fear of failure? Or do you get derailed when things don't perfectly go your way? This is the Queen getting tripped up in her shadow. If you can observe the inclinations as they arise and not fall into the old patterns, the inner Queen steps into a more joyous, fulfilled existence.

Take a moment right now, breathe deeply, and begin to name the ways in which you overly control certain areas of your life. *What makes you a control freak? What are you verbally picky about? What thoughts become repetitive and cyclical in your mind?*

If these questions are left unanswered, there will be too many layers clouding your vision. Your intuition shuts down because you have continuously not listened. If this is left unconscious for too long, you may become hardened, blocked, and unfulfilled. Joy no longer becomes accessible.

Addiction to productivity is a modern phenomenon. Often, you can't stop multi-tasking because stillness and quiet are uncomfortable. To return to stillness, silence, and not-doing might take getting physically ill or emotionally imbalanced. You don't know how to settle; it feels foreign, uncomfortable. You feel like you are not enough. If you stop, your inner judge calls you lazy, and your tricky mind replays a narrative that you don't have enough going on.

Naming the source of this tendency is essential to your personal transformation. Your inner child work is essential to understanding how this productivity or perfectionist wound plays out in your life. When you can't stop multi-tasking, and you assiduously avoid stillness, it's often because you fear your unraveling will reveal the pain of the past or present life circumstances. And this is a deeply vulnerable, often fearful, unpredictable place to be.

The drive to overdo or multi-task to the point of overwhelm makes you feel needed and wanted. It makes you feel falsely worthy in your own self, and becomes an addictive, most often empty and unsatisfying habit. This paradox of feeling good only when you are wanted or needed keeps you further away from your own experience. It muddles boundaries, alters perception of self and others, and pushes you further away from your inner power and strength.

Perfectionism breeds fatigue and anxiety. It must be separated from a job well done. Learning how to set your intention is the remedy to perfectionist tendencies—seeing the way you wish something to manifest yet letting go of the result. Leadership of any kind requires the same skill in letting go. When you are calm and clear in your mind while you are managing family and householder tasks, entrepreneurship, or corporate duties, you will maneuver through the challenges and the joys with a discerning grace.

When the invitation comes to uncover and feel what you have been unwilling to feel in the past, that is the time to stay open, welcome the deeper healing, and trust that you are on this planet to evolve.

The Queen awakens us from our slumbered trance and drama-filled pity-parties. She has no time for wasting life away nor does she diminish her leadership power. Strong spine, clear mind, the Queen is both courageous and ingenious. She is a risk-taker. She does not fear failure for she has fallen many times before. And she is acutely aware that had she not risked everything for her values and visions, her greatest treasures would have been lost.

The Initiation: Honoring the Shadow to Source Transcendence

To welcome your authentic inner Queen, you must be willing to say yes to the initiation. This requires investing in personal growth, naming the ways you abandon yourself or become hypercritical of your faults. This journey is about revealing all your hidden secrets—loneliness, unhappiness, addiction, obsession—and to receive the long-awaited support you deserve to set yourself free of lack and disconnection.

The Queen grapples with the epidemic of loneliness. It is her work to remain connected to the human realm while accessing higher levels of consciousness. Her gifts of natural leadership can make her feel separate, fatigued, and disconnected from others. The healthy Queen then retreats from her responsibilities and roles to rebalance her inner life. She returns to the simplicity and quiet of the natural world for nourishment. She gathers her dream team of humans, animals, and plant life and re-unites with the power of love to replenish her vision and remember what matters most. She returns whole and replenished.

Staying attuned to the senses—how we see, taste, touch, feel, and hear—awakens our consciousness. If we turn away from living in present-moment awareness, our senses will weaken, and so will our mental facilities. If we are constantly distracted by our cyclical thought patterns, always feeding the negative channels in our life and focusing on what we don't have instead of what we do have, we will never reach our manifestation potential. We will experience burnout and settle into the back seat of our lives wishing we had done something different.

Within each of our minds lives the potential to access deeper freedom, joy, and fulfillment. When we actively attune to the inner Queen, she awakens a higher state of universal consciousness. When we ignore her, she exhausts her dreams and lives in an imbalanced state of lost potential. However, listening to the "witness" in the mind reveals the lurking shadows that manifest as attachments and illusions in our life.

Working with the witness inside the mind is life-altering. This is how we discern the daily narrative within and see how this directs our emotions, actions and vitality. Doing this becomes the way we can heal and then discover the true source of self. Check in with your Queen as your loving witness each morning. If you realize you have gone into overwhelm, ask for her support. Receive insights from the dreamtime and be in supportive dialogue with your inner Queen. Can you open to the practice of speaking empowering and loving words to her? *"I see you are overwhelmed today—be easy on yourself."* *"I feel your grief, I acknowledge this is a challenging time. I embrace you exactly as you are today."* Not only will this feel good, but you will be subtly transformed. Your mind will shift for the good, your body will morph, and the flow of positive energy moving through you will become palpable. Furthermore, it will allow each of the feminine archetypes to grow, expand, and inform one another.

This is high-level personal work—the Queen's work. Once you begin, you will never go back. Each day becomes a living inquiry into deeper states of consciousness. This is the wellspring of manifestation and liberation. The current of bliss will come alive and bless you.

Accepting the Queen's Crown: Boundaries, Soul Care, and Courage

To accept the crown is a rite of passage. You must be willing to change your habits and perceptions of who you believe you are. It takes courage, a deep sense of self-awareness and unwavering trust to wear the robes of the Queen.

The first step is to track where you hold back or hide your feelings, emotions, dreams, and prayers. Then acknowledge your wish lists, projections, envy of others, or the tendency to put things off in fear of failure. Part of this work is to understand where you romanticize your dreams; catch yourself when you say, "When I get to this stage in my life, then I will finally get over this problem and change my life." This waiting game steals your power, takes away joy and clouds your current vision.

Take a moment right now to recall the ways in which you put off tending to your self-care. Perhaps you want to get more exercise but don't make time, or you want to meditate but keep making excuses. Maybe there is an unfinished project that is burning inside but you feel overwhelmed by it. Such inaction and projection into the future manifest as thoughts that become frustrated frequencies. Over time they become embedded in consciousness, and we begin to direct our life inside this story. At the end of the day, they make us feel defeated and despondent.

What would happen if you gave yourself permission to set these unfulfilled prophecies free? And trust that the passions, projects, and healings that are ready to come forward will arrive as they are ready? As you develop your inner Queen, do you feel a sense of relief? Perhaps you feel lighter, less guilty, and more spacious, more focused on the present moment. This is the energy of divine timing and your intuitive intelligence beginning to collaborate with you.

Healthy boundaries are part of the Queen's mastery. She catches herself when she starts to bend in ways that will only please others. She is acutely aware of when she is being manipulative and returns to her inner realms for reflective recalibration. She stays attentive to limiting core beliefs that block her vision. The Queen's boundaries are impeccable. Her "yes" does not come from past events, it arrives like a clear channel connected to her intuitive self. Her "no" comes instantly from her core, not her brain. And she doesn't second guess it. These bodily sensations are uniquely recognizable; once you have developed them, they become key to transcending and integrating the superpower of the inner Queen.

To further develop the female sovereign is to form a support team and invest in your personal growth. Choosing high level teachers, healers, and counselors to support your healing and your personal goals is life-altering. The Queen is liberated when you seek those who can meet you where you are and help you to upgrade and evolve your current situation. Her team may come in the form of her own intuition, guides, deities, or other humans.

She learns how to not fear failure; she trusts that failures of the past have transformed into life wisdom. By taking risks, she has adventured to places and received the healings that have humbled her to her knees. She has been strengthened by her vulnerability and willingness to stay authentic in the most precarious edges—from the mountain peaks to the dark caves.

The Queen's Essence

The embodied Queen is here to make great change in the world. Her ability to become vast in a microflash allows her to maneuver in critical and complex moments. This female sovereign knows that by connecting to steadiness and inner wisdom, all will be revealed in divine timing, both physically on this earthen plane and symbolically in the spirit realms.

A sense of spaciousness arrives when you surrender your attachment to how you desire a specific event or relationship to unfold. This release from constantly controlling every aspect of your life allows your mind to return to the power of love. It takes courage to be self-aware enough to understand when your own energy is affecting others in a negative way. It takes commitment to be vulnerable enough to admit when you are following a past habit or pattern.

The Queen recognizes when chaos clouds her vision. The waters become stagnant, and the air feels polluted when the stories, drama, and secrets are kept in. She understands that the pain of hiding or over-dramatizing will cost you clarity and love. She understands that hiding vulnerability keeps you cycling through past dramas and traumas.

It's human nature to ride the light and shadow aspects of daily life. The Queen takes her time when her future is unknown, or her mind is unclear. She retreats, honors her mental health, gathers options, and strategizes with her team.

Observing the impulses inside the mind is a mysterious act in and of itself. Simply witnessing the information from within is the first step in welcoming the Queen's gifts. Any insight that may come in the form of a symbol, a message, or a feeling is worthy of your attention, especially if it holds a compassionate or supportive vibration. When you are living out of fear, feeding your own resistance, or seeing from the veils of illusion, you may look to others for solutions and the capacity to source authenticity becomes lost. Your worries and fears alter how you view the world; essentially what you obsessively fear or worry about infuses your prayers and becomes your reality.

Committing to this gift of embracing the inner Queen is a journey of conscious maturation. Showing up to a devoted self-love, to a mindful and compassionate existence generates joy. Growing alongside life's changing tides is quintessential to the Queen's ability to thrive.

"I am my own muse; I am the subject I know best.
The subject I want to know better."
Frida Kahlo

The Queen Inside the Mind:
Gateway Towards Manifestation and Liberation

The mind is not only the source of our inner genius, but also the seat of our consciousness and the channel through which we manifest. It is how we find meaning and come to our understanding of who we are and where we want to go in our lives. Discovering deeply who we are, what we love, and how we want to direct our lives is the sacred work inside the Queen's temple. The way of the female sovereign is to understand how our consciousness generates our belief systems, core values and intellectual patterns.

Contemplative practices are essential to the Queen's mastery. If her mind is left unattended, she loses her virtuous way of manifestation—the way she can make change happen through intention and activation. In the center of the Queen's mind is the seed of liberation. Thoughts expand with space, visions root with time, and movements blossom with collaboration.

Discovering a sense of personal meaning in life generates wholeness. This is the key into higher states of consciousness. We receive confirmation that our gifts matter, as does the way we expand out into the universe. A simple reflective practice and prayer each morning is far more beneficial than exhausting ourselves through constant productivity. A sense of union and meaning comes through a willingness to be humble and expansive at any stage of life.

What does your inner Queen want to express? What does the Empress in your mind long for and how can you listen? In what ways are you ready and willing to take your sovereign female on a journey of liberation? Let the light shine in, pull back the curtains, open the windows in your mind. Mental clarity ignites a vision, a movement, an idea that connects to a greater force inside the cosmos. Its power will surprise you. It may feel like a fire has been stoked inside you, or like you are being guided by a force larger than yourself. This is the Queen's wizardry: her magic lives deep inside the mind.

"Remember that you are this universe, and this universe is you."

Joy Harjo

Goddess Tara: Embodied Wisdom, Pure Compassion

In the Himalayan region, especially Tibet and Nepal, Tara is revered as a high goddess or female Buddha. She is described as the wisdom goddess, the goddess of universal compassion—the mother of all Buddhas. Tara means "star" in Sanskrit; she guides her followers on their spiritual journey home like a shimmering star.

Some Tibetan legends tell of a devout Buddhist princess who lived millions of years ago. She became a Bodhisattva—a compassionate being who stays on the earth to guide others on their spiritual quest. Tara vowed to keep being reborn in the female form, as opposed to male, which was considered more advanced on the path towards enlightenment. As the legend goes, Tara stayed in meditation for ten million years, and in doing so released tens of millions of beings from suffering. Since then, she has manifested as the Goddess Tara, depicted in many different forms through art, sculpture, and legend.

She is the protectress and the cosmic creator of refined wisdom and universal compassion. Symbolic of unity, destiny, wisdom, peace, and spirituality, Tara reflects back to us our own inner wisdom. We can call upon her for sustenance and protection while enduring great challenges; she is the spark of divine creation and holds the torch of unwavering compassion in any situation.

As we sit in our contemplative practices, we can find solace and energy in Tara's ancient legacy. We invite her power to support and guide us into our unconscious minds. Here we can access the wellspring of our own healing transformation. The immanence of our authentic Queen Goddess holds radiance, power, intelligence. Through this opening, we become more attuned to the frequency of pure manifestation. We can merge with Tara's teachings to liberate our consciousness from chaos, lack or fear. We can channel her when hatred, greed, or envy begin to armor our heart and cloud our vision.

Tara's primal wisdom returns us to oneness with all of creation. Tara supports our unique transcendence in the external ecosphere while supporting our inner visions to expand out into the world. You will catch glimmers of her in the moon, and inside the extravagant fragrance of flowers. It is Tara's power that opens our minds to the constellations of the stars, reveals the distilled essence found in our unique lotus flower. Through the darkness and light of each day, Tara and the Queen merge to evolve the feminine frequency into endless compassion and brilliant courage.

The Call of Queenship:
Integrating the Art of Divine Timing

When we soften our grip and stop controling every aspect of life, a window opens into another realm. We understand the cosmic meetings, the divine timings, and the synchronistic flow that is meant to tell us something.

We can bridge worlds from our ordinary, mundane experiences to the extraordinary, mysterious, and unexplainable. With the power of the Queen, we can cultivate an openness towards receiving the great wonders of life. Fuelled by awe, embodied with a simple and sacred joy, we receive the inspiration to act inside the divine timing of this precious life.

We have all had experiences at the crossroads in life where our gut instinct told us to go one way, but our clever mind convinced us to go in a different direction. Those sudden life changes that left us feeling lost, broken, and totally disoriented—these are the pivotal moments in life that shape us.

The embodied Queen has developed a strong relationship to her inner mystic, and revels in life's great mysteries. This matrix enables her to receive the life lessons as they arrive, while trusting in her instincts, dreams, and life's mysterious coincidences. These ephemeral whispers offer supporting information for her evolution.

When we set our life intentions with clarity, while letting go of the outcome, we engage more fully in the present moment. This is the process of becoming more readily available to receive what the universe wants to bring to us. When we open to co-creating our reality with the life force that surrounds us—be it physical, emotional, mental, or spiritual—we receive deeper levels of support and energy to align with what matters most to us. This is the Queen's alchemy, which puts us in step with divine timing.

When we are connected and anchored internally, we can simultaneously read the energy in our external environment. It's as if we are presented with two frequencies daily: we can make choices based on inner listening and a felt sense; or we can ignore the messages, stay incredibly busy, or push against ourselves at the cost of our core values. When we become intentional and conscious within our daily rhythms, we begin to sense what the universe may be trying to tell us. This is divine timing.

Open your receptive channels to receive guidance and limitless joy in your daily life. Pay attention to divine timing at work. Encounters with people, nature, dreams, "aha" moments, words, synchronicities can all serve as clues to your evolving self. When your inner practices harmonize with your external life choices, you generate the ability to collaborate with your intuitive intelligence. Meditation, mindfulness, creative pursuits, time in nature, and soul care rituals are key to the virtuosity of your authentic feminine monarch. There is divine timing inside each life lesson, each experience, every encounter. Every moment of pure awareness is an initiation.

Your adult gift of empowered choice and conscious living awaits.
You get to feel, sense, decide, and direct the life that lights you up.
You decide what nourishes and activates your true nature.
This is the call of your inner Queen. This is divine timing
knocking on the door of your soul.

The Queen's Formula:
Vision to Activate

The Queen's finesse lies in discovering what you love, what lights you up, and how to formulate an action plan. How you welcome divine timing, receive intuitive downloads, and express your authentic gifts becomes your legacy.

The Queen has the capacity to ignite the flame of an idea without fear or doubt. The Queen acts upon her initial impulses and can bring her visions alive by following the sequential order inside any process she engages in. She can extract the unique essence inside any creative process and see the sequence of steps by which the vision can become fulfilled. With her intuitive channels bright, she is abundant in ideas that will enrich her craft and her community.

From conception to completion, she can see the vision in its full manifestation. She clears away the internal roadblocks by overcoming preconceived limitations. When her intentions and visions do not align, she clarifies her boundaries, distills the vision further, and adjusts her plans. She perceives when a plan needs to be abandoned or another creation may need her attention. She understands when to say no and when to say yes.

Follow the Queen's formula inside the workings of your daily life and weave it into your current projects, relationships, and adventures. Now is the time to receive clarity and to activate your visions.

Vision

If you are working with a specific project or process, welcome it into your consciousness right now. Take a moment to soften your body, attune to your breath, and see your current vision in your mind's eye. See it unfolding in its full glory—realized, manifested, solid, and real.

You must see it to believe it. With your mind–body channels alive, imagine what the vision or project completed feels like, observe the landscape and the people or energies that are present. Let this visual field land inside you. Surround it with liquid sunlight. Trust that by visualizing the creations, they are more likely to manifest because they have already come alive in your mind.

Activation

Once you visualize the manifested creation, welcome the activations necessary to put it into practice. Imagine you are already there; instead of climbing the ladder to get there, see yourself taking the practical steps you need to fulfill the vision. Be as simple and clear as possible. Observe who you imagine your team to be and sense the mind–body states you need to fulfill the vision.

Leadership and Service

Understanding the unique quality inside your vision is key to how you lead and serve. Acknowledging your gifts and your niche generates the evolution of your inner Queen. Essentially you must become your vision. This is true embodiment. Trust that you will be able to extend your offerings out into the world with clarity and confidence by embracing the work of the Queen. Make it spiritual, joyous, and infuse it with your magnetic, crystal-clear, mind–body matrix.

Reclaim your inner wild. Vision high. Diversify your personal portfolio. Shift your perception about what you can't do—it's already outdated. In your most breathtaking dreams who are you? Where do you live? Who are you with? What are you in service to? Now go live your life with this energy. Hold nothing back. The dream becomes a reality when you diversify your portfolio and live inside your visions as if you have already arrived.

Personal Sanctuary: Soul Fuel for a Fulfilled Life

The Queen creates spaces that are clear, simple, and infused with peace. Her mind gravitates towards environments with less clutter, where hints of the sacred exist. She seeks quiet. She adores listening to the birds sing, the tides roll in and out, and the wind sigh in the trees.

With the overwhelm and uncertainty of our modern existence, alongside the decreased attendance in sacred spaces, the question is "How can we create a sense of personal sanctuary, where we feel connected, peaceful, and inspired?"

Generating space within our homes that is alive with hints of the sacred is how the Queen enlivens her peace and presence. A seasonal centerpiece on the dining table, an altar that reflects the elements, a fresh bouquet, oracle cards, or relics from our ancestors—these remind us of the beauty of life. Having a journal by the bedside to capture dreams, release stressors and triggers, and express the morning and evening gratitudes naturally grows a sanctuary within. The embodied Queen is mindful of the media she consumes and is most often called to contemplative studies, artistic endeavors, and the written word as nourishment.

The Queen gravitates towards clean food, proper hydration, and a healthy balance of work, play, and study. She returns to the medicine of nature's organic sanctuaries—mountain peaks, old growth forests, the lull of the ocean's tides, the expansive sky painted with ephemeral cloud formations. The healing powers of the sun and the majesty of the starry night sky recalibrate the Queen's epic star constellation.

The grandness of Gaia takes our breath away, our sense of overwhelm and stress dissolves. When we tune in to the pulse of our natural external ecosystem, we come home to our inner self. The nervous system calms, the mind clears, and our whole body recalibrates. The Queen acknowledges when she cannot care for herself nor tend to her needs and retreats to her inner sanctum to replenish.

Living in a constant state of distraction and noise diminishes your intuitive intelligence. Practice being in silence. Self-care is the path towards building the sanctuary of love, presence, and leadership within.

The Beauty of Aging: Hone Your Craft, Live Your Wisdom

Throughout our lifetime, we maneuver through endless cycles of birth, death, and rebirth. We experience the edges of ecstasy that teach us about freedom and bliss. We suffer loss, disappointment, and the pressures that come with carrying the weight of emotional despair. We are constantly reminded of the complexity of being human. The palpable initiations of life's beginnings and endings become essential to our own evolution.

The embodied Queen becomes the wild Empress who takes great pride in aging with grace. Not only that, but she loves herself more each year that she cycles around the sun. Each journey involves pearls discovered, pain released, secrets liberated, healings ignited. Each wrinkle earned becomes another beauty mark. She chooses how she wants to age; she makes her own rules as to what defines beauty.

She reclaims her inner wild child with the flare of the Maiden, the deep love of a Mother, the wisdom of the Sage, the strength of the Huntress, the sensuality of the Lover, the vision of the Mystic, and the refined mind of the Queen. She is magnetic beyond measure. Her spark is electrifying, her mind clear of judgement, her heart a deep sea of bottomless compassion.

Aging invigorates her passion for life. Her devotion to her craft becomes bolder, more refined. She holds nothing back. Her intuition, creativity, and sovereignty generate the life she always knew was meant for her. She freely releases her outdated attitudes, heartbreaks, and drama-queen ways in order to dance with the wild Empress within. This infectious energy is like a living oracle, a sacred vision. Aging wisely is a gift.

Wild Freedom:
A Visualization to Empower Aging

It's up to you to reframe your perceptions on aging.

Take a moment to place your hand on your heart and reach the other hand towards the sky. Breathe deeply, anchor yourself towards the earth, welcome in the vast skies above.

Make a decree to shift your beliefs about aging. All your dislikes, fears, moans, groans, pity parties and negative impressions—give them up. Speak to them out loud or journal them. They are outdated anyway. Observe how you feel when you begin to name your fears around maturation.

Aging with a wild, free, and expansive attitude opens more doors than you can ever imagine.

Remember, you get to live your life in wild freedom.

This is the new feminine way.

Are you ready for this journey?

Get curious about what your life would be like if you let go of your attachments to how it should look or feel. Journal about your experience. Name at least one call to action that will support you in radically loving your whole self.

Curiosity and Queendom

Curiosity generates an inner listening, which essentially activates your intuition. Through this attitude, you build trust and solidarity in your own mind–body channels. You can more readily access the doorways into your essential nature—your soul self. The core of your inner spirit unifies.

The matrix of your inner reserves, past lives, ancestral imprints, and lived experiences comes alive and wants to be expressed. Building, creating, moving into the wild river of life as opposed to swimming upstream—this life is yours to be fully lived. The good girl martyr princess is ready to expand her story. She is ready to give it all to the dance of life and shape-shift into the best version of herself. Once you awaken your inner Queen, you will never lose her again. She will walk you to the river and purify your vision. Her healing powers will instill joy, love, expansion, and clarity into every area of your life. The river stones await your crossing into Queendom.

Welcoming presence, compassion, and accountability into everything you do will build up your intuition. You no longer need to abandon your gut instincts in the name of leadership or love, or because you feel you should do something or be like someone else. You empower your journey through a process of inner listening.

You get to live with an unapologetic self-worth while navigating by your instincts. Honoring your intuitive process is one of the greatest gifts you can give yourself on your earthside adventure.

We Are the Divine Feminine of the Planet

Can you visualize your body as an instrument of love? Is it feasible that you have arrived on this planet to be the wisdom carrier of love? Could you be here at this time to evolve our human heart to that of star, planet, universal alchemy, creative intelligence? This is how the divine feminine manifests.

Picture a loving, deeply wise grandmother sitting before you, counseling you to let go of the limitations of your fixed identity and live from a deeper truth. This grandmother has arrived to anchor you into the limitless frequency of love. Her energy is what will heal our world.

Now is the time to begin this journey, to release your fixations on what you don't have, but rather see what you do have. Now is the time to feel what you have been unwilling to feel. This is a healing path. Your inner child is brave enough to face the shadows of the past. Hold her hand, the grandmother wisdom will guide you in the darkest of nights and the brightest of days.

Now is the time to ignite the divine feminine archetypes—the Maiden, Mother, Sage, Huntress, Lover, Mystic, and Queen—as the stars inside the core of your soul constellation. We, the divine feminine of the planet, are here, standing in solidarity with your prayers, witnessing your mighty grace, embracing every tear, fear, doubt. Together we hold the cries inside the holy Mother Earth. She summons our hearts to rise. It's time to move towards a higher collective consciousness of love. You will never regret answering the call to journey deep into your own karmic unfolding. Where you will take it is yours to determine.

May we begin, dwell, and return to this quintessential divine feminine with every breath we take. May we be reminded of the unforgettable, unnameable power of love that is the infinite source of creation.

A grip over the heart loosens.
Her gaze expands, surprising, foreign and delightful.
Hummingbird medicine, eagle vision, true nature unfurling.
A radiance inside her own virtuosity, her moon's crown aglow.
An exquisite field of wildflowers bloom—unforgettably her own.

An honoring of the matriarchs that have come before—
and those who will come after.
Give yourself wholly to this steady force of love.

The healing songs arrive in the most auspicious moments.
This is the divine working its magic, blessing our lives,
and giving us faith to carry on.

We, you, me, us—let us carry this feminine reign forward.
For the novel has ended—
and a new story begins.

Practices for Embodying the Queen

Guided Visualization:
A Journey to Ignite Your Soul's Code

Intention
Recalibrate your mind–body channels, reveal the deeper wisdom gifted to you in this lifetime.

Materials
Journal, candle, comfortable and warm space to lie down, relaxing music if supportive.

Read through this visualization first before guiding yourself or others on this journey.

Light a candle, set a clear intention to nourish your mind–body channels and to receive supportive insights to enhance the quality of your life. Journal about three or more things that you are ready and willing to let go of in your life. Now write down three or more gratitudes/prayers/intentions.

Find a comfortable space to lie down, make sure you are warm, and place a scarf over your eyes. Begin by tuning into your breath: each inhale connects you to a sense of warmth, each exhale releases thoughts in the mind or stress in the body. If your body needs to stretch or move to get more comfortable, follow the impulse.

When you are ready, constrict or tighten all the muscles in your body: clench your fists, feet, shoulders, face, and torso. Then release your body fully with a deep exhale. Repeat this three times.

Now, slow down your breath: inhale for a count of four, hold your breath for four counts, then exhale fully for six counts, and hold your breath for 2 counts. Repeat this technique at least six times, or until you are fully relaxed.

Let us now begin the journey to ignite your soul's code.

Attune your visual field to a lighthouse in the near distance. See the power of the waves crashing against it. There is a warm, alluring, and mysterious essence to this land and seascape. Intrigued, you follow the path to get there, soaking in the rugged shoreline, already feeling free and nourished by the scents, sounds, and life of this area.

As you arrive, the lighthouse door swings open. Upon entering, you look up and become awe-struck by the spiraling staircase lined with ancient texts of every color, size, and shape.

A momentous feeling surges through your body, your mind instantly expands into deep time. You know you have arrived here for a reason. Your hands touch the books as you walk up the spiraling staircase. Each one has its own unique feeling, weathered by a timelessness that goes beyond its written words.

You land upon one book that feels deeply compelling. It almost jumps out of the shelf for you to receive it.

You pause, breathe deeply, and hold the warmth of this knowledge in book form against your heart. As you open it, its captivating words land inside your consciousness—this is your soul code. This text is meant for you only. It is part of your service to the world. It holds the alchemy of your own karmic unfolding. Lifetimes of healing transpire in this moment. Your soul code has the deepest formulas needed at this time in your life.

You may receive a message, an affirmation, a symbol, an image, a landscape. Merge with this field of consciousness. Let it formulate and land deep inside your body. A repeating code may present itself to you. Receive what wants to come through. Trust the first glimmers or flashes that arrive. Soften your whole being to collect the treasure of this journey.

Bring your awareness back to the center of your body. Take six deep breaths in and out. Gently stretch your body. Roll into a fetal position on your left side. Seal-in the wisdom received.

Thank yourself for choosing to connect in this conscious field. Journal about your experience.

The Queen's Formula: A Visioning and Activation Practice

Intention

*To shine the light on your intuitive callings and
craft them into activation.*

What is the most compelling project, vision, or intention currently inside of you? Journal about it, and then refine it into one sentence. It may be supportive to generate an "I am _____" or "I will _____" statement.

Vision

You must see it to believe it. What does this vision or goal feel like? Why is it coming forward now? What do you already know about this vision and why is it kindred to you?

Come up with one sentence to embody what you are visioning or calling into you at this time. It may be supportive to begin with: "I am calling in _____ as I know this will feed my soul."

Activation

What are the practical steps needed to align with your vision? What daily practices can you commit to bring this vision into clarity in your mind? Who is your support team?

Leadership and Service

What is the unique quality or teaching inside your desire? Acknowledging your gifts and your niche is a creative process. You will be able to extend your offerings out into the world with clarity and confidence. To embrace the work of the Queen is to enhance the quality of your life. Embody this frequency as a daily undertaking.

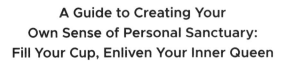

A Guide to Creating Your
Own Sense of Personal Sanctuary:
Fill Your Cup, Enliven Your Inner Queen

Intention
*Nourish your body–mind channels to enhance the quality of
your life and be in greater service to your vision.*

In Nature

Find an outdoor sanctuary or a "sit spot"—a place where you can find solace in nature, and to which you can easily return. Leave your phone at home and practice the art of witnessing your surroundings. Be in silence. Take in the colors, sounds, scents. Notice the shifts in plant and animal life during the different seasons. If possible, go to your "sit spot" one or more times weekly. This becomes a sanctuary for the soul, a nature immersion that brings you peace and rejuvenation.

At Home

Create an altar in your home—with a candle, plant, crystals, images, positive affirmations, etc. Recreate your altar each month to encourage inspiration and connection to what is meaningful to you. Keep your home clutter free and clean. Find one space in your home that is your personal sanctuary.

In Your Mind

Begin with a daily gratitude journal practice. Include your dreams and your successes in letting go—the art of shedding negative self-talk is powerful.

By tracking your thoughts, you become more self-aware; you can catch yourself when negativity begins to take over your life. Journal about your thoughts and redirect them.

In Your Body

Spend time in nature, move your body, get proper rest. Stay current with what kind of movement or exercise feeds your soul and nourishes your body. Get to know what kind of food best serves your lifestyle. Food is love; so is getting good sleep. The most powerful practice is to lower stress levels, and to learn how to let self-love become your baseline. You are always evolving; staying present with your current needs is essential to finding the sanctuary within.

The Discipline of Practice:
Seven Days of Ascension, Your Inner Queen Activated

Intention

*To connect with your highest self and welcome your inner
Queen. Release habitual patterns that no longer serve you.
Inspire your mental capacity in alignment with your dreams.*

Materials

*Seven days of commitment, an open mind, and a journal
or a friend to share your experience.*

Begin by committing to seven days of physical, artistic, or spiritual practice that you know will serve your inner Queen. It may be the gym, studio, wood, ocean/lake/river, the meditation cushion or the yoga mat, or hydration or food intake. Commit to seven days of practice that will transform you by its regularity. Show up every day to this practice. Make a star chart, put it in your calendar; whatever it takes, make it happen.

Pay attention to what makes you resist your intention, and what makes you activate it.

This is all part of getting to know the conscious and unconscious aspects of both our light and our shadow. We need both to be fully realized to meet our own whole, full, inspired inner Queen.

Journal Prompts to Awaken Your Inner Queen

The Embodied Queen's Characteristics
Articulate | Humble | Courageous | Confident
Impeccable | Visionary | Strategic

How do you nourish your inner Queen?

When you imagine your best life, what comes forward? Who is there? What are the conditions? What are you doing or not doing?

What can you shift in your daily life to meet, inspire, and embody your inner Queen?

Write a mantra or affirmation that holds the essence of what you desire to activate currently in your life. Repeat it to yourself frequently.

Journal Prompts to Work with the Queen's Shadow

Shadow Characteristics of the Queen
Critical | Overly Analytical | Manipulative | Egotistical
Perfectionistic | Short-sighted

What are the repetitive thoughts that cycle in your mind? Observe and name the thoughts that are on the negative spectrum.

Who is the "roommate" or the "inner judge" inside your mind? Where does she come from (family of origin or current life systems)? How does she control you? Can you become more aware of her voice? Name her repeating thoughts.

Describe the ways you meet your own inner Queen's shadow.

How does perfectionism, the desire to control or the fear of failure hold you back from doing what you want in your life?

What practices, or techniques bring your shadow towards the light?

What daily call to action can you commit to in order to shift the narrative of unworthiness, or lack—and welcome in the Queen's abundance and leadership?

Be All of You for You—for Us

Look up, the moon will guide you.
Nothing to hide or prove.
You are not too much or too little.

Believe in your wholeness,
your inner wild is your superpower.
Be all of you for you – for us.

Breathe it all in.
Savor the pause inside the pause.
Generate reverence for the hardships and the joys.
The divine whispers in the most unassuming moments.

Navigating life's rugged terrain, tears of truth
Glimmer in her myriad of waxing and waning forms.
The once unreachable, the questionable – now
steppingstones up spirit mountain.

The Weaver

"Your soul is a seeker, lover, and artist; shape-shifting through archetypal energy, between your darkness and fields of light, your body and spirit, your heaven and hell, until you land in the moment of sweet surrender; when you, as a dancer, disappear into the dance."

Gabrielle Roth

Chapter 8

The Weaver's Work

Integrating the Soul Wisdom
of the Feminine Archetypes

The weaver never knows the final creation.
Yet you begin with a passion that burns as bright as the sun.
The poet never knows what words will fall onto the page,
yet your calling to express is all consuming.
Singer, dancer, storyteller, sculptor—
you just take a giant leap of faith.
Catch the fleeting snapshots of shadow to light.

The wonder missions, the deep-sea dives.
The path up spirit mountain is rugged.

Unravel the threads bound into your artist's spirit.
Have courage to sit with the loom, weaving the world's complexities
until they become answered prayers.
Hand to paintbrush, songbirds at dusk, salted ocean tears—
heart shatters into a million pieces.
Yet somehow the threads find their way home.
Spinning, looping, braiding, they become intertwined—
gifting us with ancient love songs.
Whole, wild, rugged, and powerful beyond measure.
A single strand has the potential to transform the world.
Open, soft, wildly inviting—
the womb of the divine feminine births the world awake.

The Weaver's Work

A Weaver lives inside each one of us. Like an archetypal artist at work, she invokes each day as a unique creative process. She awakens her own brilliance with these deep-sea questions: "What am I evolving into today? What are the teachings ready to be received? How can I offer my love and presence into the world more fully?"

The Weaver resides inside the heart of the divine feminine matrix—like the spiral inside the ancient fossil, the elegant center of a flower in full bloom, or the celestial origin of a star's antiquity. This divine essence is the frequency found inside the Weaver. Open your visual field and imagine the Weaver inhabiting the center of your body. From this central Weaver frequency streams all the other archetypes. The Weaver occupies the center of your soul. The archetypes are the threads with which the Weaver creates your living tapestry.

The Weaver spins many web-like creations in her lifetime. Dedicated to living her highest, most fulfilled, and liberated version of herself, she is the essence of truth. She holds infinite love and forges the bridge between the physical and otherworldly dimensions. She is a living embodiment of courage. Her power is as immense as the great mother ocean, her devotion to her life's work makes mountains move.

Naturally we are born whole, with complete access to the Weaver's wisdom. Part of our personal evolution is to reclaim this entirety and tap into the alchemy of each archetype. Through all its unique, wild, rugged, and refined forms, the work of the evolved feminine way is to take a seat at the Weaver's loom and weave the life you desire.

Collecting, sifting, and entwining the distinct characteristics of the female archetypes generates the divine feminine incantation. Our daily inspiration and affirmation becomes "life as a living ceremony." A ritualistic, reverent, and lush current runs through each archetype. Each one finding her authentic expressions, motivations, and articulations as we engage with a life lived to its most precious meaning and highest purpose.

The Maiden's infectious zest, the Mother's generative abundance,
the Sage's healing powers, the Huntress's warrior spirit, the Lover's
depth of intimacy, the Mystic's intuitive capacity, and the Queen's
clear channel for inner power and wisdom—these characteristics
are ready to be activated. Integrate them as resources to recognize,
heal, and generate the life you are meant to live.

The Weaver holds the entirety of this potent alchemy.
With each cycle, adventure, and experience in life, call upon
the Weaver to guide you. Call upon her to support your visions,
to spin your prayers into the cosmic web of life.

Greet your fears with a wildly magnetic, deeply compelling love.
The Weaver knows your power, she trusts your instincts, let
her come alive. Give her a face and a name. Sing to her, sit in
silence with her, make poems in her honor. Allow her riveting
spirit to weave your life with an elegance that is fierce,
and a devotion to the highest goodness in all living beings.
Have faith, return to your source, nourish the most fulfilled
version of yourself—to the stars and beyond.

Reclaiming the Feminine: Now Is the Time

We are at a time of reclaiming the feminine. When you embody
the highest expression of your soul's calling, you have embraced the
divine feminine in all her most expansive forms. We are waking up
as a collective—women and men, children and elders. There is a
vast movement towards developing the archetypal qualities of the
feminine. We are learning to reveal, integrate, and fulfill our original
gifts, free of societal, cultural, or inherited limitations.

Beyond gender, each of us has the capacity to develop both
feminine and masculine energies. Only thus can we embody our
true potential and live with joy and peace inside this gift of life. The
higher work is to observe the shadows that derail us from our path,

to learn from the imbalances that overtake our reality, and hold us inside our undeveloped potential. This naturally feeds unhappiness and a sense of not fully inhabiting the true power within. Let us source the positive qualities of our masculine history and work on releasing the imbalances.

The world's inability to value the feminine and acknowledge its essential voice on the planet right now is perpetuating the problem. Half of the circle of humanity is excluded from power. Undermining the feminine leaders of the world is closing doors to a sustainable future where justice and equality reach those who are suffering. From an environmental point of view our house is on fire. We can no longer live as we used to. If you are not understanding the repercussions upon the next generation, you are living in illusion.

Politically, women are ready to lead their countries out of war and into peace. Socially, the feminine holds the power to see beyond bias and bring out the best in humanity. Physically, women still bear the future generations of the world. Emotionally, the evolved feminine understands when she is coming from reactivity and works to respond from her inner impulse. This leads to her capacity to lead, live, and love from a grounded, balanced, and intuitive awareness.

Women are the life givers, the holders of intuitive power. In songs, stories, and language they have passed down the wisdom from our ancestors to our children. Each archetype is woven into the fabric of a women's matrix—Maiden, Mother, Sage, Huntress, Lover, Mystic, and Queen—like strands of silk ready to be spun into wholeness.

No time is lost; we are never too old to revision our life and begin anew. The daily weave of life becomes the sacred journey. We land inside our true nature by understanding how to unravel from inherited family systems, by actively seeking counsel and support as the self-talk and narrative becomes small and self-defeating. True leadership is founded on the awareness of which archetype is ready to come alive within, ready to be seen and heard, ready to transform and evolve.

The practice is to begin and end from a place of love. Honoring your lived experience and the braided wisdom collected along the way gives voice to your own sovereignty. The acknowledged and nourished living archetypes become the sacred turning points in which you get to create, emote, and shape the life you desire.

Never underestimate the power of your own intuition. By tuning in daily, your vision will become vast, connected, and steady.

Coming Home: The Archetypal Journey

Like a gardener observing the plant cycles of birth, death and rebirth, the archetypes will reveal areas of excess and lack in your life. Once you become aware of these imbalances, they can be honored and met with compassionate curiosity. Here, the deeper healing has begun. Saying yes to the soul work of the archetypes gives you the power to choose what works and what doesn't. Some doors will instantly close; trust that those weren't meant for you. Other doors will easily swing open and instantly welcome you home.

Doing the work instills powerful confidence in the body and mind. You don't have to second-guess your trajectory or trip over your own limitations, because you have cleared the path. Then the fun begins: you get to follow the trail in joyful liberation towards the sanctuary of your soul. This comes with a deep inner knowing and a refined reflection of your own evolutionary process.

The work keeps you connected to what matters most. You become a steady force of goodness and right action. You no longer need to hide behind fake identities and false personas in order to please people. Choices stream from the bold yes over the old games of maybe, could have, should have, blame, guilt, and shame. By sourcing your own liberated and authentic ways, you become less fatigued by your inner conflicts and more guided towards the potency of the divine feminine.

You no longer fear your power, nor are you afraid to fail or fall. You are the enchantress of re-discovery and re-invention. You know it's never too late to create anew, to revision the vision, to be the shape-shifter in life. With this conscious frequency of daily living you feel real; your self-love expands and blossoms into the next cycle of your own becoming. You anchor into your own light expansion. Enlivened by wonder you generate spaciousness and a compassionate grace that shape-shifts your physical body and magnifies wholeness.

Organically, you follow the call to birth your next monumental creation into the world. You give yourself to it freely, trusting that the process—from planting to full expression—is essential to your personal development. The Weaver and all her archetypes under-stand that she must get out of the way of her own ego. The embodied feminine leaps from steppingstone to steppingstone on her archetypal journey.

"The land knows you, even when you are lost."
Robin Wall Kimmerer

The Weaver's Craft: From Form to Spirit

To awaken and form a relationship with each feminine archetype is a life-altering gift. Weaving the feminine archetypes is an endless path towards self-discovery and freedom. The ones who weave are the ones who heal. The Weavers are the creators, bringing together art and spirituality, into leadership for a wholesome world. The metaphor of weaving is an ancient way of understanding the universe—melding the spiritual and physical planes, the emotional and intellectual capacities, and the personal and collective energies.

As a physical act, weaving involves the crossing of two threads; one horizontal and one vertical; two threads must be bound to complete the design. The opposites are woven together to create the whole. This is the quest of the divine feminine. Gathering the threads of grace and challenge, of joy and complexity inside our everyday existence is the Weaver's work. Like an artist, her craft is to create something from nothing. To discover the potential in each new creation, completely unique from any other piece. Symbolically, the Weaver attunes her senses to receive the life codes that come into her consciousness. To set them into motion by letting them come alive, named, created, manifested, refined, honored, and eventually released into freedom.

The Weaver's magic does not get diminished by life's complexities; rather she utilizes the wisdom inside each archetypal configuration to choose her threads wisely and weaves her work with the depth of many lifetimes back and many lifetimes forward. Like the grandmother cedar tree who spends eight hundred years weathering changes under and above ground, she is resilient beyond measure. Meeting each season and cycle of plant, animal, and human life, she becomes the home to all. The Weaver holds the medicine of a wise grandmother spirit. She speaks many languages: that of the earth, and the birds, the plants, the waters, and animals, stars, sun, and moon.

The Weaver is the seeker and keeper of cosmic knowledge. She is simultaneously timeless and time itself. She is form and formless, chaos and peace. She is pure consciousness. The Weaver is the atmospheric artist at work, weaving the power of the elemental forces—earth, air, fire, water, and ether—into her loom. Sourcing from the wisdom of her ancestors, pulling out what no longer serves her or humanity. The Weaver will take you to the holy waters, purify your vision, liberate you. You will meet her at the precipice of your life, she will catch you when you fall and guide you as you push beyond your own limitations. This is the medicine of the Weaver. She is the alchemy of your wildest dreams. Her power lives inside you. She weaves the languages of all the female archetypes into a unified constellation.

The Weaver's message is timely and essential. Receive her wisdom, let the Weaver grace your home and family. Invite her into your own mind–body channels daily. See the bottomless sea of goodness within yourself. Feed your soul with a purely authentic weave that attracts all that you want to create in your life. Connect with the image of a colorful woven tapestry, filled with the symbols and prayers that you know will attract and expand your dreams. Feed it daily with your attentive care and a depth of self-love that goes beyond the fast pace of ordinary life.

Resourceful beyond measure, with a heart of gold, the Weaver lives her own deeply wise, complex, and ancient tapestry. Her way of endless compassion and infinite love is her superpower. She stops to give the homeless person what she can and is of service wherever she can be. She is forgiving and understanding when others are acting out of their shadow, because she has the wisdom to know the archetypes at work. She takes nothing personally. She returns to her loom and steadily discovers the depth of her soul's work on this planet. Her creations evolve as she does. Steady as the seasons, she explores her next body of work, ready to greet the next adventure of joy, peace, depth. She inspires others to embrace life to its fullest. Through the history of her precious existence on this earth, she walks with a love that gets brighter, richer, and ever more abundant.

Silence is a gateway to access your creative impulses.
A mind–body frequency of flow, grace, and communication
becomes a living, breathing process of creativity.
When you give it space and time, it may touch upon the
mysterious, ephemeral, undiscovered.

New thoughts, ideas, insights are generated from stillness,
silence, and the present moment.
Trusting in the compassionate forces of spiritual evolution
evokes deep vulnerabilities.
It moves us in ways that the ordinary life does not.
The Weaver prayerfully and artistically offers
her body of work to the world.

The Weaver's Code: Life as a Living Ceremony

When you engage in your life as a living ceremony, you become an expression of present-moment brilliance. You no longer fear change. Rather you engage in the power of self-transformation as part of your daily soul work. You are the artist, writer, poet, storyteller, healer—weaving your way through freedom of expression. You trust that the doors opening for you are the doors of your own awakening. The Weaver understands she is co-creating and collaborating with the divine. To let your inner wild woman out to play is to know your power and to love your soul. Your passion, creativity, and radiance arise from a higher consciousness; a deeper healing is happening on the planet. Walk your soul path, invite all the archetypes to join you—this is the practice of a lifetime.

Reclaim your inner wild. Vision high. Diversify your personal portfolio. Shift your perception about what you can't do, or who you are not—it's already outdated. In your most breathtaking dreams, who are you? Where do you live? Who are you with? What are you in service to? Now go live your life with this energy. Hold nothing back. The dream becomes a reality when you expand your matrix and live inside your visions as if they have already arrived. Maiden, Mother, Sage, Huntress, Mystic, Lover, Queen—each archetype timelessly woven into your wisdom body. This evolved feminine way holds the distilled essence of the Weaver's potency: she is ready to be ignited, sourced, and activated at any stage in your life.

When a woman embodies the strength and love of the sacred feminine archetypes, every single person on this planet benefits.

The Weaver initiates each day with prayers of gratitude and compassionate curiosity. Your adoration of the natural world nourishes your spirit. You seek beauty and amplify love through dedication to your craft. You tend to your authentic self daily—listening, nourishing, and accepting your inner child. You are the healer, enchantress, creatrix—the artist living with a sense of awe and wonder, seeing the bottomless love in all forms. With profound courage you venture to the edges of your light and your shadow. With vulnerability and humility, you no longer fear failure or falling. You have met your own dark nights of the soul; you understand that death is another form of rebirth.

Integrating the mind–body channels and welcoming the glimmer of spiritual awakening is the healing catalyst within the new feminine way of leadership on this planet.

You must be willing to say goodbye to your old self and step into who you are today. Your unique essence is ready to emerge, to do good work for the betterment of humanity and this planet, and to set the new paradigm of the evolved feminine frequency into motion.

When you slow down enough
to hear the raven's wings flap,
speak to the roses as they unfurl their sensuous petals,
hug trees, walk barefoot in the forest—
each day is a thread in the fine silk weave of your
empowered feminine spirit.
Now breathe into this cherished life.

Appendix
Rituals and Wisdom Practices
to Embody the Archetypes

Chapter 4
Practices for Embodying the Huntress

Chapter 5
Practices for Embodying the Lover

Chapter 6
Practices for Embodying the Mystic
Guided Visualization:

Chapter 7
Practices for Embodying the Queen
Guided Visualization: A Journey to Ignite

Index

About the Author

Photo by Kornelia Kulbackie

Mara Branscombe is a mother, writer, yogi, artist, teacher, mindfulness leader, ceremonialist and spiritual coach. She is passionate about weaving the art of mindfulness, self-care, creativity, mind–body practices, and earth-based rituals into her life and work, and she has been leading community ceremony since 2000.

An adventurous spirit, Mara has sailed across the Atlantic Ocean, trekked across the Himalayas, studied yoga in India, planted trees in Canada's north, lived off the grid in a remote cabin in the woods, worked as a Waldorf (Steiner School) teacher, and then found her passion for dance and choreography. All the while yoga, meditation, mysticism, and ritual have been at the heart of Mara's journey. Her trainings in the Incan Shaman lineage and the Pagan tradition have greatly inspired her life's work of earth-based, ceremonial, intentional, and heart-centered living and loving.

The author of *Ritual as Remedy: Embodied Practices for Soul Care*, Mara currently lives in Vancouver, Canada, with her husband and two daughters.

For more information visit: **www.marabranscombe.com**